KV-637-905

ESSENTIAL
CHINA

Written by Graham Bond and Paul Mooney
Revised and updated by James Howard

© AA Media Limited 2012
First published 2008. Information revised and updated 2012

ISBN: 978-0-7495-7080-4

Published by AA Publishing, a trading name of AA Media Limited, whose registered
office is Fanum House, Basing View, Basingstoke, Hampshire RG21 4EA.
Registered number 06112600.

Colour separation: AA Digital Department
Printed and bound in Italy by Printer Trento S.r.l.

Find out more about AA Publishing and the wide range of services the AA provides by
visiting our website at theAA.com/shop

A04463
Mapping © MAIRDUMONT/Falk Verlag 2011
Additonal data from Mountain High Maps® Copyright ©1993 Digital Wisdom, Inc
Transport map © Communicarta Ltd, UK

About this book

Symbols are used to denote the following categories:

✚ map reference to maps on cover
✉ address or location
☎ telephone number
🕐 opening times
💷 admission charge
🍴 restaurant or café on premises or nearby
🚇 nearest underground train station

🚌 nearest bus/tram route
🚈 nearest overground train station
⛴ nearest ferry stop
✈ nearest airport
❓ other practical information
ℹ tourist information office
➤ indicates the page where you will find a fuller description

This book is divided into five sections:

The essence of China pages 6–19
Introduction; Features; Food and drink; Short break

Planning pages 20–33
Before you go; Getting there; Getting around; Being there

Best places to see pages 34–55
The unmissable highlights of any visit to China

Best things to do pages 56–69
Great places to have lunch; places to take the children; stunning views and more

Exploring pages 70–185
The best places to visit in China, organized by area

Maps All map references are to the maps on the covers. For example, Yangshuo has the reference
✚ 2K – indicating the grid square in which it is to be found

Admission prices
Inexpensive (under 30RMB)
Moderate (30–100RMB)
Expensive (over 100RMB)

Hotel prices Prices are per room and per night excluding breakfast:
$ inexpensive (under 500RMB);
$$ moderate (500–1500RMB);
$$$ expensive to luxury (over 1500RMB)

Restaurant prices Average prices for a meal for two excluding drinks:
$ inexpensive (under 100RMB);
$$ moderate (100–250RMB);
$$$ expensive (over 250RMB)

Contents

The essence of...

Few countries have developed as rapidly as China since the 1980s. In Beijing, Shanghai and Guangzhou the transformation has been almost complete. Yet the age-old traditions of the Chinese remain largely intact, despite the influence of modernity. Any country with a continuous civilization of more than 3,000 years is certain to be packed with history, while a nation the size of China is bound to offer an almost unmatched scenic diversity. From pagodas to serene mountain tops, from fairytale karst peaks to crumbling outposts of the Great Wall and magnificent imperial palaces, China offers a unique and enthralling travel narrative.

features

A story is often told to visitors about Arthur Waley (1889–1966), the eminent translator who introduced Chinese literature to Western readers for the first time in the early 1900s. Having never visited China, Waley resolved to sail there to see the land he knew so intimately in his mind. When his boat reached harbour in China, Waley apparently had second thoughts. The translator suddenly realized the China of his imaginings would bear no resemblance to the land he was about to set foot on. Waley decided not to disembark and sailed back to England a few days later having never set foot on Chinese soil, but with his idyllic images of China still intact.

Many visitors to China may find that they share Waley's concern. The China they experience will bear little resemblance to the one seen in movies or read about in books. China is a country of sharp contrasts. Walk around an isolated village and you'll see satellite dishes poking from crumbling tiled roofs. Yet nearby farmers manually irrigate fields in much the same way as their grandfathers did. China continues to grapple with the problem of how to preserve its ancient past, while providing its people with the modernity and comforts they crave.

GEOGRAPHY

- China covers an area of 9.6 million sq km (3.7 million sq miles). The country is bordered by Russia and Mongolia to the north, North Korea to to the east, Vietnam, Laos and Myanmar to the south, and India, Pakistan, Bhutan, Nepal, Afghanistan, Tajikistan, Kyrgyzstan and Kazakhstan to the west.
- The country of China comprises 22 provinces, five autonomous regions and four independent municipalities.

Hong Kong, a British colony since 1841, was returned to China in 1997, and Macau, settled by the Portuguese in 1557, was made a part of China again in 1999.

CLIMATE

● Because of the size of the country, there are great variations in climate and temperatures, from Siberian conditions during the winter in the far north to tropical humid weather in the south, and desert conditions in the northwest. The best times to visit are spring (April–May) and autumn (October–November).
● Travellers are advised to wear layers of clothing in the winter and light clothing in the heat.

PEOPLE

● China has a population of approximately 1.3 billion people. Some 92 per cent of the population are Han people, or ethnic Chinese, with 8 per cent belonging to one of the 55 different ethnic or linguistic groups.

● Most Chinese speak Putonghua (Mandarin), the official national language based on Beijing dialect. Chinese ideographic writing is the same everywhere.

CHINESE NAMES

● Chinese surnames traditionally precede the given name and this is the system used in this book. It is customary to address people by their surnames followed by Xiansheng (Mr), or Xiaojie (Ms). For younger people, including tour guides, it is common to precede the surname with the familiar title "Xiao", or little, ie Xiao Wang.

THE ESSENCE OF CHINA

food & drink

China has a wide variety of regional cuisines, with each province having its own speciality. The following are the more popular cuisines that can be found around the country.

BEIJING

Mild, but hearty. Wheat, rather than rice is the staple and dumplings, breads and noodles feature prominently. The most famous dish is Peking duck. The meat and crisp skin of the duck and sliced spring onions or cucumbers are wrapped in thin crêpes of slightly griddled, unleavened dough dabbed with sweet soybean paste. Soup made from the duck bones is also delicious.

SICHUAN

Spicy and richly flavoured, this cuisine makes liberal use of hot peppers. Popular specialities include *gongbao jiding* (cubes of chicken sautéed with chillies), *suancai yu* (fish and cabbage in soup) and *mapo tofu* (diced bean curd with ground pork, garlic and chilli). Don't overlook the *chongqing huoguo* (Chongqing hotpot), a fiercely hot concoction that can banish the cold of the bitterest winter.

HUNAN

The Hunanese are also known for their liberal use of chilli peppers. Hunan was the home of Chairman Mao Zedong; China has many restaurants specializing in the favourites of the former leader.

JIANGZHE

The highlight of this cuisine (from Jiangsu and Zhejiang, two provinces located on the east coast), is seafood. This style is also known as Shanghai-style cooking.

CANTONESE

Cooking from Guangdong Province in southern China is lighter and less sweet compared to other cuisines. Cantonese food is perhaps most famous for the breakfast and lunchtime snacks known as dim sum, or *dian xin* in Mandarin. Waitresses wheel carts loaded with steam baskets through the restaurant and diners select what they want from the parade of dumplings, pastries and roasted and steamed treats.

MUSLIM FOOD

Across China, Muslim chefs cook up lamb kebabs, *nang* (flat breads) and countless spicy lamb and beef dishes. Tasty *lanzhou lamian* (Lanzhou pulled-noodles) can be enjoyed across the land.

VEGETARIAN

Called *su cai,* vegetarian dishes have long been a part of Chinese cuisine and contrary to popular opinion, are anything but bland. This cuisine is served at Buddhist temples and restaurants around the country.

ETIQUETTE

Chinese dishes are ordered communally, with guests helping themselves from the collection placed in the centre of the table. It is good manners to take from each dish what can be eaten immediately; do not accumulate a great pile of food on your side plate or in your rice bowl. In many restaurants there is no side plate, and so you are expected to use the rice

bowl as the resting place for food taken from the communal dishes. If there is a serving spoon or chopsticks, use them to select your chosen dish; otherwise it's acceptable to use your chopsticks to take food directly from the communal plate. Watch your Chinese friends or neighbouring diners and act accordingly. It may be acceptable to sip soup directly from your soup bowl if others are doing so.

ALCOHOLIC DRINKS

Virtually all restaurants – unless they are Muslim – serve beer or spirits made from either sorghum or rice. Imported spirits and wines are usually only available at more fashionable restaurants and bars.

BEVERAGES

While tea *(cha)* is the standard beverage served at meals, restaurants also serve a wide variety of soft drinks, mineral waters, juices, and alcoholic beverages, including an increasingly wide variety of wines in better establishments. Coffee is rarely served in restaurants, except Western eateries, but cafes can be found everywhere. Another popular drink is bubble tea *(nai cha)*, a sweet, milky tea (originally from Taiwan) containing dark balls of jelly.

DRINKING ETIQUETTE

When dining in a more formal setting, guests usually do not drink individually. It is considered polite to wait for the host or another guest to toast you before drinking from your glass. You may also like to offer a toast to others sitting at the table. Make eye contact with your intended target and raise your glass with two hands, tipping it slightly in his or her direction. After taking a drink, hold out the glass in the direction of the person to show how much you've consumed. It's common for Chinese friends to try to get you to drink a lot, and you will often hear the toast *ganbei*, or "bottoms up". If you don't like to finish your drink in a single gulp, you can just say *suiyi*, or "how you wish", which means either party can drink as much as the person likes.

short break

If you only have a short time in which to visit China and want to get under the skin of the country and of Chinese culture, here are some essentials:

● **Wander around a park** early in the morning for a look at how Chinese start their day. You'll see people doing ballroom and disco dancing, callisthenics and martial arts.

● **Go fly a kite:** kite flying is a favourite pastime among youngsters and senior citizens and takes place in large open spaces, such as Tiananmen Square (➤ 83) in Beijing.

● **Visit a karaoke parlour:** while many Westerners are put off by the idea of performing at a karaoke, it's a national pastime for the Chinese. A good voice is not required.

● **Enjoy Peking duck** at one of Beijing's numerous duck outlets. Spread the thin pancake with plum sauce, layer with spring onion or cucumber, and stuff with crispy pieces of skin and meat.

野生鸡

试吃

● **Ride a bike:** with Chinese city streets becoming increasingly clogged with private cars, the bicycle remains the most stress-free means of sightseeing. Be warned, drivers are not known for their consideration for cyclists.

● **Visit a Buddhist temple:** see the Chinese worship as they have done for centuries, lighting incense and kneeling before Sakyamuni and assorted bodhisattvas.

● **See an opera:** different regions boast their own operatic styles, but all feature melodramatic plots, highly stylized acting and magnificent costumes.

17

● **Take the train:** share a bag of sunflower seeds and a cup of cha with the locals during a train ride to one of your destinations. Soft-sleeper berths accommodate four people in a closed room, while hard-sleeper berths have six beds in an open cubicle.

● **Shop in a market:** most Chinese pick up what they need at market places, where you can haggle, prices are generally lower and stalls overflow with choice.

● **Visit a tea house:** finish off the day with a visit to a traditional tea house, where tea is slowly brewed in tiny pots.

Planning

Before you go

WHEN TO GO

JAN	FEB	MAR	APR	MAY	JUN	JUL	AUG	SEP	OCT	NOV	DEC
1°C	4°C	11°C	21°C	27°C	31°C	31°C	30°C	26°C	28°C	9°C	3°C
34°F	39°F	51°F	70°F	81°F	88°F	88°F	86°F	79°F	82°F	48°F	37°F

High season   Low season

Temperatures listed are the average daily maximum in Beijing. China's climate varies massively from region to region. Deepest winter can be bitterly cold and summer is often witheringly hot – both seasons should be avoided if possible. Beijing is extremely cold in winter and very hot in summer. Shanghai has a mild winter but an extremely hot and humid summer. Hong Kong is invariably warm and sticky, but cools off over the winter months. Only Yunnan, in southwest China, has a genuinely pleasant year-round climate. Summer is probably the least pleasant time to travel in China, because of the temperatures and the crowds. If you can bear the chill, there's much to recommend travelling in late autumn or early winter. Avoid Chinese New Year holidays (January/February), Labour Day holidays (first week of May) and National Day holidays (first week of October).

WHAT YOU NEED

● Required
○ Suggested
▲ Not required

Contact your travel agent or embassy for the current regulations regarding passports and the Visa Waiver Form/Visa. Your passport should be valid for at lest six months beyond date of entry.

	UK	Germany	USA	Netherlands	Spain
Passport/National Identity Card (Valid for 6 months after entry)	●	●	●	●	●
Visa	●	●	●	●	●
Onward or Return Ticket	○	○	○	○	○
Health Inoculations (► 23, Health Matters)	○	○	○	○	○
Health Documentation (► 23, Health Matters)	▲	▲	▲	▲	▲
Travel Insurance	○	○	○	○	○
Driving Licence (national or International Driving Permit)	N/A	N/A	N/A	N/A	N/A
Car Insurance Certificate	N/A	N/A	N/A	N/A	N/A

WEBSITES

www.en.gov.cn
www.cnto.org
www.ebeijing.gov.cn

www.shanghaiist.com
www.discoverhongkong.com
www.thebeijinger.com

TOURIST OFFICES AT HOME

In the UK

CNTO (China National Tourist Office)
71 Warwick Road
London SW5 9HB
☎ (020) 7373 0888

In the USA

CNTO 350 Fifth Avenue, Suite 6413
Empire State Building
New York, NY 10118
☎ (1 888) 760 8218

HEALTH MATTERS

All visitors are strongly recommended to arrange medical insurance before leaving for China; this should include transport home. Medical facilities are good. Most tourist hotels should be able to recommend a good dental clinic. Any treatment will need to be paid for in advance and then reclaimed on insurance.

Inoculations Typhoid, hepatitis A, diphtheria and rabies are all potential issues in China and anyone concerned should seek medical advice prior to travel. Malaria is present only in rural parts of Guangxi, Hainan, Yunnan and Guangdong; assuming you are limiting your travel to major tourist areas and big cities, there's little risk, but check with your travel clinic.

TIME DIFFERENCES

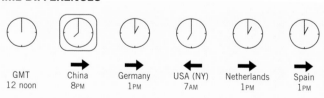

GMT	China	Germany	USA (NY)	Netherlands	Spain
12 noon	8PM	1PM	7AM	1PM	1PM

China is eight hours ahead of Greenwich Mean Time (GMT+8). The whole country officially lies within the same time zone, though Xinjiang, in the far west, operates local hours two hours behind Beijing Standard Time. Daylight saving time is not used, meaning China is seven hours ahead during the summer.

PLANNING

NATIONAL HOLIDAYS

1 Jan *New Year's Day*
Jan/Feb *Chinese New Year*
(7 days)*
8 March *International*
Women's Day
5 April *Qingming Festival*

1–3 May *Labour Day*
Holiday
1 June *International*
Children's Day
1 July *Birthday of the*
Chinese Communist Party

1 August *People's*
Liberation Army Day
Sep/Oct *Mid-Autumn*
Festival*
1–7 Oct *National Day*
Holiday

*Governed by the lunar calendar

WHAT'S ON WHEN

January/February *Chinese Lunar New Year:* the most important holiday of the year for the Chinese begins on the first day of the lunar calendar's first moon and lasts for seven consecutive days. Families come together to enjoy special meals and to light fireworks, and lively temple fairs are held in major parks. Some shops and restaurants may operate limited working hours or even close, especially in more remote areas. However, most urban centres will remain busy. Indeed, shopping and eating are two of the most popular leisure activities for families during this holiday.
Lantern Festival: this popular celebration, marking the end of the Spring Festival, falls on the 15th day of the first lunar month. Some people buy paper lanterns and walk through parks and streets with them illuminated.
The Tibetan Lunar New Year: falls in January, February or, occasionally, March and is marked by archery and horseback competitions, religious dances and other ceremonies.
Guanyin's Birthday: marks the birthday of Guanyin, Buddhism's Goddess of Mercy, on the 19th day of the second moon.

April *Qingming (Tomb Sweeping) Festival:* traditional holiday when Chinese tidy and decorate the burial places of their ancestors.
Water Splashing Festival of the Dai Nationality: this "minority" festival takes place 13–15 April in Xishuangbanna, southern Yunnan province, and involves dragon-boat races, fireworks and water fights.

May *May Day Holiday (1–3 May):* International Labour Day is now celebrated in China as a three-day holiday. This is not a good time to travel in China, as travel and hotels can be difficult to reserve.

May/June *Dragon Boat Festival (May/June):* commemorates the death of Qu Yuan, a patriot and poet who drowned himself as an act of political protest. The day is marked by dragon-boat races and the consumption of *zongzi* (bamboo leaves stuffed with sticky rice and a meat or bean filling). *Children's Day (1 June):* teachers, parents and children go to parks and on field trips.

August/September *Mid-Autumn Festival (15th day of the 8th moon):* celebrates a 14th-century uprising against the Mongols. People present friends with Mooncakes, and gather outside to stare at the heavens.

October *National Day Holiday (1–7 October):* commemorates the founding of the People's Republic of China. The government has designated this a week-long holiday, designed to encourage domestic tourism and spending. It's probably the worst time to travel in China.

Event Listings For up-to-date information on where to eat, shop and play in Beijing, Shanghai and Guangzhou check out *City Weekend* (www.cityweekend.com.cn), a free bi-weekly English magazine. In Beijing, look out for *The Beijinger* (www.thebeijinger.com) and *Time Out* (www.timeout.com/beijing). In Shanghai, grab a copy of *That's Shanghai* or *Time Out*. In Guangzhou, look out for *That's PRD* and in Hong Kong, *HK Magazine* and *bc magazine*.

Getting there

BY AIR

Beijing Capital International Airport

25km (15.5 miles) to city centre

🚇 30 minutes

🚌 40 minutes

🚗 30–60 minutes

Pudong International Airport

40km (25 miles) to city centre

🚇 8 minutes

🚌 60 minutes

🚗 40 minutes

Hong Kong International Airport

40km (25 miles) to city centre

🚇 22 minutes

🚌 50 minutes

🚗 40 minutes

Beijing Capital International Airport (www.bcia.com.cn) has six major Airport Bus routes (7am–11pm) into the city. Airport Express trains runs every 15 minutes to Sanyuanqiao and Dongzhimen, both on the metro. A taxi ride into town will cost around 80RMB.

All long-haul international flights to Shanghai land at Pudong International Airport (www.shairport.com). There are seven main Airport

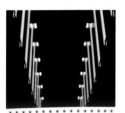

Bus routes into the city (7:30am–11pm). The Maglev (Magnetic Levitation train) whisks passengers the 30km (19 miles) to Longyang Lu metro station in eight minutes (7am–9pm). Taxis to the city centre cost around 160RMB.

Hong Kong International Airport (www.hkairport.com) is located around 40km (25 miles) from Hong Kong Island. Buses, trains and taxis make the trip, though the Airport Express train is the most convenient method, speeding to Kowloon or Hong Kong Island (Central) in around 20 minutes.

BY TRAIN

It's possible to arrive in mainland China by train via several routes. The Trans-Siberian from Moscow crosses the Russia-China border at Manzhouli, in Inner Mongolia, before stopping at Harbin and Beijing.

The Trans-Mongolian enters China at Erenhot, also in Inner Mongolia, before heading onto Beijing. Apart from trains to Pyongyang, the only other international link is with Hanoi. There are twice-weekly services from Beijing to the Vietnamese capital, though a change of train is required at the Vietnam-China border. In all cases, customs formalities are completed at the border and passengers are required to disembark.

Hong Kong has direct train links with the mainland along three routes, Beijing, Shanghai and the Guangdong city of Zhaoqing (stopping at Guangzhou en route). The trains pass directly through the Hong Kong-China border and customs formalities are completed on arrival.

Getting around

PUBLIC TRANSPORT

Internal flights Planes are more expensive than trains but the difference is often negligible. Tickets are often discounted, but full price may apply at weekends and busy times.

Trains China's rail network is excellent and is the country's main means of transportation. There are soft sleeper berths (four people sharing a cabin) and hard sleeper berths (six people sharing a section in an open car).

Buses Bus services are widely used within and between towns and cities, although the quality and comfort varies sharply. Buses are generally viewed as less safe as highway conditions are often poor, seat belts are scarce and traffic can be chaotic.

Ferries Ferries run from Hong Kong to Macau, Zhuhai and Shekou as well as other towns on the Pearl River. Ferries also run from Shanghai to the island of Putuoshan and from Yantai to Dalian. Ferry services run along the Yangzi River, but these have decreased in number. River ferries run between Guilin and Yangshuo on the Li River.

FARES AND TICKETS

Trains Obtaining tickets is difficult in China. It is cheapest to buy them at the station, but crowds are heavy. For a surcharge, you can buy a ticket through your hotel or at ticket offices in town. Depending on the route, you can reserve up to 10 days in advance. It is often possible to upgrade on the train.

Air Though travel agents can help buy tickets it's possible to book cheaply online using web-based aggregators (www.ctrip.com or www.elong.com). International credit cards can often be used, though there are sometimes problems processing payment.

Buses and ferries Tickets are plentiful and can be booked from the departure point.

TAXIS

Taxis are cheap and convenient. Few drivers speak English, so it's advisable to have your destination written in Chinese, and to always carry a business card from your hotel with its address in Chinese. Patronize only taxis from the line in front of the main doors of the airport terminal.

DRIVING

- Conditions on Chinese roads seem chaotic to outsiders. The concept of right of way doesn't exist and it's common for drivers to pull out in front of oncoming vehicles. Expect the unexpected at all times. (See Car Rental, ➤ 29.) Alternatively, you may wish to hire a driver and car.
- Speed limits on intercity expressways: 120kph (75mph); on urban express roads: 100kph (62mph); on urban roads: 70kph (43mph); on single-lane urban roads: 30kph (19mph).
- It's compulsory for drivers and passengers to wear seat belts on highways, though this is rarely enforced.
- Breaches of the rules often go unpunished, although if a driver is stopped, offences will usually be punished with a fine.

CAR RENTAL

Renting your own car is only possible in Beijing, Shanghai, Hong Kong and Macau, but you are only allowed to drive within the city's boundaries. Taking taxis remains a cheaper and easier option for many of China's visitors. It is possible to pick up a temporary Chinese driving licence at Beijing Capital Airport and Pudong International Airport, on presentation of your driving licence. Be aware, however, that conditions on roads in Shanghai and Beijing are dangerous for drivers who are novices to China.

Being there

TOURIST OFFICES

Beijing, Shanghai and Hangzhou have a network of tourist information centres, as well as dedicated tourist "hotlines". However, throughout China the quality of information and levels of English are often poor, although Hong Kong is an exception.

Beijing There are several information centres throughout the city. Beijing Tourism Hotline ☎ (010) 6513 0828.

Shanghai There are several information centres dotted around the city. Shanghai Tourist Hotline ☎ (021) 6355 5032.

Hong Kong Hong Kong has superb tourism information facilities. There are Hong Kong Tourism Board information counters at Hong Kong International Airport. There is also a multi-lingual tourist information hotline: ☎ (852) 2508 1234; www.discoverhongkong.com.

MONEY

The renminbi (RMB) is the main unit of currency in China. It's also known as the yuan and referred to in speech as "kuai". It is divided into 10 jiao. Notes are in denominations of 1, 2, 5, 10, 20, 50 and 100RMB. The Hong Kong dollar (HK$) is the currency of Hong Kong and the pataca (MOP) is the currency of Macau. All three currencies are roughly equal in value, though the renmimbi is maginally the strongest and the pataca weakest.

Major credit cards are accepted in many places in China's larger cities and most airports and city banks have facilities for changing foreign currency and travellers' cheques. It's possible to obtain cash from nearly all Bank of China ATM machines using international debit cards.

TIPPING

It is useful to carry plenty of small notes
Yes ✓   No ✗

Restaurants (if service not included)	✗	
Bar Service	✗	
Taxis	✗	
Tour guides	✓	5–10RMB per day
Hotels (chambermaid/doorman etc)	✗	
Porters	✓	5RMB
Hairdressers	✗	
Toilets	✗	

Tipping is officially discouraged in China, but tour guides and staff at hotels who carry bags will often expect a small tip. Some restaurants may include a 10–15 per cent service charge in the bill.

POSTAL AND INTERNET SERVICES

Post offices Times vary, though 9am–5pm, Mon–Sun, is a rough guide. The airmail rate for postcards is 4RMB. Airmailed letters cost around 5RMB to Europe, USA and Canada, though the price depends on weight.

Internet services China has become as extremely wired nation in recent years. Most hotels offer Internet access though prices are relatively expensive. Dark and smoky Internet cafés infest China's towns and cities though finding them can be tricky and most are not signed in English. Look out for shopfront pictures of cartoon characters or fantasy warriors.

Prices costs from as little as 2RMB per hour. Coffee shops in bigger cities often have complimentary computers and many offer free wireless access for those with laptops.

TELEPHONES
Public telephones are hard to find sometimes. Calls cost 5 jiao for a local call. IP cards can be purchased at newspaper booths for long-distance calls.

International dialling codes
Dial 00 followed by:
UK: 44
USA/Canada: 1
Irish Republic: 353
France: 33
Germany: 49

The dialling code for mainland China is 86 (applies from Hong Kong or Macau)
The dialling code for Hong Kong is 852 (applies from the mainland)
The dialling code for Macau is 853 (applies from the mainland)

Emergency telephone numbers
Police: 110   Fire: 119   Ambulance: 120

EMBASSIES AND CONSULATES
UK ☎ (010) 5192 4000
Germany ☎ (010) 8532 9000
USA ☎ (010) 8531 3000

Netherlands ☎ (010) 8532 0200
Spain ☎ (010) 6532 3629

HEALTH ADVICE
Sun advice Central and southern China can be hot and sticky, while the north is extremely dry. It is easy to become dehydrated. It's also easy to burn at higher altitudes in western China, especially Tibet.

Drugs Pharmacies sell much of the same range of everyday medicines you would find in Western Europe or America but they are rarely labelled in English. There are English-speaking pharmacists at some clinics in the larger cities, but prices for medicine at foreign clinics can be steep.

Safe water Tap water in China is not safe to drink and must be boiled before drinking. Bottled water is widely available at restaurants, small shops and kiosks. It is not advisable to walk barefoot in rice paddies or other wet areas.

ELECTRICITY
China's power supply is 220 volts. Plugs come in a variety of sizes and shapes, and most sockets accept at least two varieties. Most modern plugs are two-pin, similar to those used in the USA. Hong Kong uses the same three-pin plugs as the UK.

PERSONAL SAFETY
China is relatively safe, and although theft is rare, you are advised to take the usual precautions. Pickpockets are common on crowded city streets and on buses, so place your passport and wallet in a safe place. In public places keep a close watch on your bags and other valuables. There is a lot of counterfeit money in circulation in China, so do not change currency with money exchangers on the street.

OPENING HOURS

- Shops
- Banks
- Museums/Monuments
- Post Offices
- Pharmacies

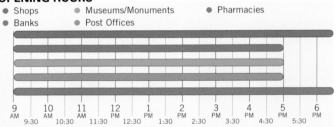

Department stores open around 10am and usually close at 10pm. Markets open as early as 3am and are finished by 8am, others stay open later. Hong Kong shops may not open until 11am but generally stay open very late. Banks open daily, though some services may not be available during the long lunch break (11:30am–2:30pm) and on weekends.

LANGUAGE
On the whole few Chinese speak English, although many will be enthuastic to speak to you. Chinese characters are rendered into the Latin alphabet by an official system known as pinyin. Most sounds are composed of an intial and a final. Sounds are largely pronounced as written, but note the following:
Initials c as the "ts" is cats; j as the "j" in "jeep" but slightly sharper; q as the "ch" in cheap but slightly sharper; r has no English equivalent

and is pronounced as a cross between y and r; x as the "sh" in sheep but with the s given greater emphasis; z as the "ds" in lids; zh as "j" in jam. **Finals** a as the "ar" in car; e as the "er" in her; er as "are" in are, with a vocalized final r; i as "ee" in feet unless preceded by c, ch, r, s, sh, z, zh when it is pronounced as the "er" in her, but with no exhalation; o as "war" in war; u as the "oo" in cool; ai as "y" in sky; ei as "ay" in play; ao as "ow" in cow; ou as as "o" in so; en as "un" in under; ie as "ye" in yes; ia as "ya" in yard; un as "on" in won.

hotel	*fan dian*	how much is it?	*duo shao qian?*
guest house	*bing guan*	room	*fang jian*
do you have a room?	*ni you mei you fang jian?*	bathroom	*xi shou jian*
		toilet	*ce suo*

how much is this?	*zhe ge shi duo shao qian?*	3	*san*	10	*shi*
		4	*si*	11	*shi yi*
too expensive	*tai gui*	5	*wu*	20	*er shi*
inexpensive	*bu gui/pian yi*	6	*liu*	30	*san shi*
0	*ling*	7	*qi*	100	*yi bai*
1	*yi*	8	*ba*	1,000	*yi qian*
2	*er*	9	*jiu*		

rice	*fan*	pork	*zhu rou*
noodles	*mian tiao*	shrimp	*xia*
fried rice	*chao fan*	soup	*tang*
egg	*ji dan*	fruit	*shui guo*
fish	*yu*	boiled water	*kai shui*
duck	*ya*	tea	*cha*
chicken	*ji rou*	coffee	*ka fei*
beef	*niu rou*	beer	*pi jiu*

aeroplane	*fei ji*	taxi	*chu zu che*
airport	*fei ji chang*	bicycle	*zi xing che*
bus	*gong gong qi che*	I would like to go...	*wo yao qu*
bus station	*gong gong qi che zhan*	Where is the...?	*...zai nar?*
train	*huo che*	I would like a ticket	*wo yao mai piao*
railway station	*huo che zhan*		

hello	*ni hao?*	I don't understand	*wo bu dong*
goodbye	*zai jian*	Do you understand?	*ni dong bu dong?*
How are you?	*ni hao ma?*	yes	*shi*
Well, thank you.	*hen hao, xie xie*	no	*bu shi*
thank you	*xie xie*	I like...	*wo xi huan*
When?	*shen me shi hou?*	I don't like...	*wo bu xi huan*
No problem	*mei you wen ti*	today	*jin tian*
What is this?	*zhe ge shi shen me?*	yesterday	*zuo tian*
I understand	*wo dong*	tomorrow	*ming tian*

Best
places
to see

1 Bingmayong (Terracotta Warriors)

www.bmy.com.cn

During a drought in 1974, farmers digging a well discovered one of the most amazing archaeological finds in modern history – the terracotta warriors.

The terracotta army – thousands of soldiers, horses and chariots – had remained secretly on duty for some 2,000 years, guarding the nearby mausoleum of Qin Shi Huang, the first emperor of the Qin Dynasty. Known as the Huangdi, or Yellow Emperor, Qin ruled from 221–206BC and is credited for unifying China for the first time. He is also remembered for his ruthless destruction of Confucian books and slaughter of his enemies.

Each of the terracotta figures – some standing, some on horseback, and some kneeling, bows drawn – is unique, with a different hairstyle and facial expression. Three pits have already been dug at the site in Lintong county, 37km (23 miles) east of Xi'an. Pit No 1 is home to about 6,000 life-size terracotta figurines in a military formation marching east. Pit No 2 contains hundreds of chariot drivers, horses, cavalrymen and infantrymen. Pit No 3 is thought to be the army headquarters.

Qin's mausoleum lies 1.5km (1 mile) to the east of the terracotta warriors, and it is believed that a much larger terracotta army and valuable cultural relics lay buried in the tomb. Hu Hai, the second Qin Emperor, reputedly mandated the

sacrificial burial of all the builders and
childless imperial maids. Visitors are
permitted to walk around the site, but
it has yet to be excavated owing to the
construction methods originally used
to build the tomb, which make it
impossible to excavate safely using
current techniques.

➕ 2F ✉ Shaanxi Province, 37km (23 miles)
from Xi'an 🕐 Mar–Nov daily 8:30–5:30;
Dec–Feb 8:30–5 ✋ Moderate 🚌 Buses
from Xi'an Railway Station 🚉 Xi'an Station
✈ Xi'an International Airport

2 Changcheng (The Great Wall)

The Great Wall was one of mankind's most splendid achievements. The ruins extend across northern China.

Dating from the Qin dynasty, the Great Wall was created when Emperor Qinshi Huangdi linked together a formerly disparate array of lesser walls. Today, their remains creep in segments across China from the North Korean border to the harsh deserts of Xinjiang. The bulk of the wall is in ruins while other sections – principally those around Beijing – are over-restored: the best sections lie somewhere in between.

The Ming paid particular attention to the wall, cladding it in brick and making it a more stalwart fortification. Despite Ming engineering, the Manchu were invited through the pass at Shanhaiguan and proceeded to install themselves as rulers over China for two and a half centuries. The most accessible and crowded tourist sections are Badaling and Mutianyu. If you are reasonably fit,

the four hour walk from Jinshanling to Simatai is far more exciting. For views, the best section around Beijing is at Jiankou. Alternatively, head west to Jiayuguan Fort in Gansu province, for some of the most astonishing images of the wall against snow-capped mountains and desert.

✚ 1E–5D ✉ Badaling, Yanqing county; Jinshanling, Miyun county; Mutianyu, Huairou county; Simatai, Miyun county; Jiayuguan, Gansu province ☎ Badaling (010) 6912 2222; Mutianyu (010) 6162 6505; Simatai (010) 6903 5030 ✋ Moderate 🍴 Restaurants at entrance points ($–$$) 🚌 Badaling: Buses from Qianmen, Beijing Railway Station and Deshengmen. Mutianyu: No 6 bus from Xuanwumen or Dongsi Shitiao. Simatai: many hotels arrange day trips by bus; Jiayuguan: short taxi trip to the fort from Jiayuguan town 🚉 Badaling: 623 from Beijing Station

3 Chang Jiang (Yangtze River)

Rising in the icy mountains of Qinghai Province, the Yangtze passes through seven provinces, ending its journey in the East China Sea close to Shanghai.

The Yangtze, at 6,380km (3,956 miles) in length, is the third longest river in the world, dividing China between the wheat-growing north and the rice-growing south. Every bend in the river evokes stories from history and mythology, such as Kublai Khan's crossing of the river on his conquest of the Song dynasty in the 13th century.

Most Yangtze cruises begin at Chongqing and head downriver in the direction of the Three Gorges Dam. Many of the towns once visited by the cruise ships are now under water thanks to the reservoir created by the dam. The river was first dammed across its entire width in 2003 and the Yangtze has been on the rise ever since. Now that the waters have reached their full height, the Three Gorges

are 105m (114yds) shorter than they previously measured.

Still magnificent, the gorges, located on a 200km (124 miles) length of the river between Baidicheng and Yichang, are crowded with towering peaks, jagged cliffs and caves. Qutang Xia is the shortest, but most dramatic, of the three. Wu Xia, or Witch Gorge, is surrounded by sloping forests and mysterious mountain peaks. Xiling Xia, the last and longest, is marked by shoals and rapids.

At "New" Wushan travellers can disembark for an excursion through the Three Lesser Gorges of the Daning River, riding the waters through almost surreal scenery.

Approaching Yichang, the cruise boats pass through the five colossal locks of the Three Gorges Project. Once you reach the other side, you can climb atop the dam, 185m (607ft) high. Yichang is now the stopping point for most river cruises.

✚ 1H–5G ✉ Central China

🍴 Cruise ships serve food 🛳 Boats from Chongqing to Yichang (3 days, 2 nights)

❓ Tours can be arranged through the China International Travel Service (CITS) and international travel agencies. Note that a variety of boats can be booked, from simple steamers to expensive cruise ships.

4 Gugong (Forbidden City)

www.dpm.org.cn

Established between 1406 and 1420, the Forbidden City remains the most complete collection of imperial architecture in China.

With around 9,000 rooms, the Imperial Palace (Forbidden City) is the largest palace complex in the world. Home to China's emperors from 1420 to 1911, the palace has been rebuilt many times, but has always retained its original design. The wall that surrounds the complex, anchored at the corners by four guard towers, is encircled by a moat. The palace is divided into three sections: the palace gates, principal halls and inner court.

After passing through the Gate of Heavenly Peace (Tiananmen) and the Upright Gate you reach the Meridian Gate, the traditional entrance to the Forbidden City. Only the emperor was permitted to enter the Forbidden City. Beyond this you will find the final portal, the Gate of Supreme Harmony.

Designed to accommodate 90,000 people during ceremonies, the outer courtyard leads to the Hall of Supreme Harmony where important ceremonial occasions were observed, including the emperor's birthday. Behind stands the Hall of Middle Harmony, where the emperor dressed for functions, and the Hall of Preserving Harmony.

Within the inner courtyard the Palace of Heavenly Purity, Hall of Heavenly and Terrestrial Union and Palace of Terrestrial Tranquillity were used for lesser functions. The Palace of Terrestrial Tranquillity was where the emperors consummated their marriages.

The smaller courts in the east and west are where the imperial families, concubines and attendants lived. Behind this can be found the Imperial Garden.

✚ *Beijing 5c* ✉ Xichangan Jie, Beijing ☎ (010) 6513 2255
🕒 May–Sep daily 8:30–4; Oct–Apr 8:30–3:30 💶 Moderate
🍴 Café northeast of the Hall of Preserving Harmony ($); toilets in the palace grounds 🚇 Tiananmen East or Tiananmen West 🚌 1, 2, 4, 10, 20, 52, 57, 101

5 Hong Kong

A British colony from 1841 until it was returned to China in 1997, Hong Kong is the ultimate example of East meets West.

Hong Kong is a bustling city of contrasts where glistening skyscrapers dwarf small temples and bustling produce markets. Cross Victoria Harbour on the Star Ferry for a spectacular view of the skyline. Outside the Star Ferry Terminal (Pier 7) in Central, board the 15C bus to the Peak Tram Station for the steep vertical ascent to Victoria Peak. Once on the Peak you can enjoy a bird's-eye view of the harbour and city below and then take a gentle stroll along one of the surrounding paths. The view is stunning and well worth it, though air pollution often blurs the view during daylight hours. Jump on a double-decker bus (get a seat on the upper deck if you can) for the spectacular roller-coaster ride to Stanley where you can browse colourful market stalls or walk along the beach. Visit one of the floating seafood restaurants in Aberdeen for some delicious and fresh seafood.

The "Heritage Tour" will take you to the area between the Kowloon Hills and mainland China, a diverse rural and suburban region where you will visit traditional temples, homes, markets and a picturesque walled village. A 40-minute ferry ride will whisk you from the booming Central district to one of the many serene offshore islands where

you'll see fishermen patiently tending their nets and farmers working in the fields.

Head to Lantau Island to visit the Po Lin Monastery, home of a huge seated Buddha. Stay on the island for a vegetarian lunch at the temple and then continue your visit to the nearby fishing village of Tai O. Or for a more active option take a boat out to Yung Shue Wan in the north of Lamma Island and walk along the trail past spectacular views from the hills all the way to Sok Kwu Wan at the island's waist. Finish your journey with an inexpensive seafood meal by the water in Sok Kwu Wan as the sun goes down.

➕ 3L ✉ Southern China 🚇 Mass Transit Railway (MTR) links all districts 🚌 Bus and tram services 🚉 Kowloon–Canton Railway (KCR) ⛴ Star Ferry ❓ The Heritage Tour is run by the Hong Kong Tourist Board (852) 2508 1234.

6 Lhasa and Tibet

The spiritual, cultural and political centre of Tibet. All devout Tibetan Buddhists hope to make a pilgrimage to this holy city at least once.

The Potala Palace is the largest and most complete palace complex in Tibet. It was built in the seventh century, but was destroyed by war in the ninth century. The present structure, located on a hill overlooking Lhasa, was built in 1645 by the fifth Dalai Lama. It is divided into two sections, the White and Red Palaces. The White Palace, built in 1653, is where Dalai Lamas administered government affairs. In 1690, eight years after the death of the fifth Dalai Lama, a local regent decided to build a funerary pagoda to house his remains, and work was begun on the Red Palace. This palace, located between the eastern and western wings of the White Palace, is decorated with a gilded copper roof, and includes chapels, shrines and the tombs of former Dalai Lamas. The inner room of the present Dalai Lama's apartment has been left just as it was on the day he fled to India in 1959, moments before the People's Liberation Army arrived to reinforce Chinese rule over Tibet. Paintings are an important part of the palace, consisting of murals, thankga, or Tibetan painted scrolls, and other decorations.

The nearby Jokhang Temple is always crowded with pilgrims and is famous as the home of one of the most precious Buddhist images in China, the

Sakyamuni Buddha. The statue was brought here from China by Wen Cheng, a Tang dynasty princess who married the Tibetan King, Songsten Gampo. The main hall has a set of murals portraying Princess Wen Cheng's arrival in Tibet.

✚ 10R ✉ Provincial capital of Tibet ⏰ The Potala: daily 9–4. Jokhang Temple: daily 8–12:30 (interior temples) 🚌 Buses and minibuses cover the city 🚆 From Beijing, Shanghai, Chongqing, Chengdu, Lanzhou and Xining ✈ From Beijing, Chengdu, Chongqing and Xi'an ❓ All foreign visitors need a Tibetan Travel Permit to enter Tibet

Lijiang

Nestled in the lee of the snow-capped Jade Dragon Mountain, Lijiang, with its ancient canals and traditional architecture, is one of the best-preserved old towns in China.

Lijiang is one of the few towns in China to survive the wrecking ball that has transformed much of the rest of the country. Old wooden houses with tiled roofs face the thick cobblestone streets. Canals criss-cross the town, accented here and there by quaint stone bridges. At intervals, steps descend to the surface of the water where indigineous Naxi

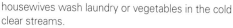

housewives wash laundry or vegetables in the cold clear streams.

Lijiang, one of 33 UNESCO World Heritage Sites in China, is divided into two parts. The old town, although often very busy with tourists and visitors, is the place to visit. The brick and timber structures are marked by falling eaves and wooden slats carved with various auspicious symbols. The fronts of the houses are covered by ornately carved panelled wooden doors. However, the rows of beautiful old shops have traded their traditional wares for souvenirs. Chinese restaurants sell traditional delicacies next to Western coffee houses serving burgers, fries, milkshakes and brownies. If you want to beat the crowds, get up very early, delve into the alleyways behind the main streets, or head up into the hills for panoramic views.

Naxi society was traditionally shamanistic and structured along matriarchal lines. The Naxi have unique music and dance traditions, which add to the town's rich cultural *mélange*. Local musicians give evening performances of the ancient music of Lijiang, which is believed to be a form of Taoist music that spread here in the Song Dynasty. The Naxi are also known for their unique written language, one of the last pictographic scripts in existence today.

✚ 12S ✉ Yunnan Province, 196km (122 miles) from Dali 🚌 No vehicles are allowed in the old city, which can be easily covered on foot. Buses for Lijiang can be taken from Kunming and Dali ✈ Daily scheduled flights leave from Kunming. There are also direct flights from Chongqing, Chengdu and Shenzhen and regular flights from Beijing, Shanghai and Chengdu

8 Mogao Ku (Mogao Caves)

The Mogao Grottoes of Dunhuang house a rich collection of Buddhist sculptures and frescoes.

In the Han dynasty, Dunhuang was an important Buddhist centre because of its position at the junction of the northern and southern tracks of the Silk Road. It was under Tibetan control from 781 to 847, when there was an intense rivalry for control of the trading routes across Central Asia. The caves date from the fourth century, and the site is among

the most impressive along the Silk Road. It's said that a Buddhist monk had a vision in which he saw 1,000 Buddhas. He began to carve grottoes into the sandstone cliff, and was later joined by other monks and craftsmen, who filled the caves with Buddhist images.

There were originally up to 1,000 caves, of which 492 survive, filled with about 2,400 clay statues. Murals dating back to the Northern Wei Dynasty show the strong influence of Central Asian Buddhist traditions. Of special significance is cave 17, which houses a huge collection of paintings, manuscripts and textiles spanning six centuries. It provides invaluable evidence for the history and development of Chinese art. However, as tourism takes its toll, the number of caves open to the public is dwindling.

✚ 11P ✉ 25km (15.5 miles) southeast of Dunhuang, Gansu Province ✪ May–Oct daily 8:30–6; Nov–Apr 9–5:30 ✋ Expensive 🚌 Buses from Dunhuang. Hotels also arrange transportation 🚆 Trains run to Lanzhou and Urumqi; for Beijing you will have to travel first by bus to Liuyuan ✈ Dunhuang Airport ❓ Visitors must be accompanied by a tour guide (included in the ticket price). Photography is strictly forbidden in the caves. Bring your own torch, or rent one at the entrance.

BEST PLACES TO SEE

9 Qingdao

Qingdao retains strong echoes of its German past in its buildings and brewing.

Qingdao, or Green Island, is one of the most beautiful port cities in China. The city was just a small fishing village until Europeans began to take an interest in it in the mid-19th century. The Russians made it their winter anchorage in 1895, and the Germans turned it into a foreign concession in 1897, using the murder of two Catholic missionaries as a pretext. The Germans gave the city a makeover during their 17-year rule, building Bavarian-style mansions, churches and a train station. Qingdao was then divided into European, Chinese and business districts. The town was given to the Japanese under the Treaty of Versailles in 1919, but was finally returned to China in 1922.

A walk through the streets reveals the city's German heritage. Huaishilou, a castle-like structure, once served as the German governor's residence. The double-spired Catholic church, near Zhongshan Road, and the Protestant church, opposite Xinhaoshan Park, are excellent examples of German architecture, as is the Bavarian-style Xinhaoshan Hotel, adjacent to the park.

One of the city's most famous institutions is the Tsingtao Brewery (this is the older spelling of the city's name). The brewery was founded in 1903 by the Germans, and continues today to brew its distinct German recipe in the original copper stills.

Qingdao is also known for its six beaches and fresh seafood – an ever-prominent part of Shandong cuisine.

➕ 5E ✉ Shandong Province 🍴 Seafood restaurants can be found along the seafront area ($–$$) 🚌 No 6 bus covers most of the city's major sites 🚆 Trains to Beijing, Ji'nan and Shanghai 🚢 Boats to Shimonoseki (Japan) and Incheon, South Korea ✈ Qingdao Airport ❓ Beer Festival, August

10 Yangshuo

With its amazing karst formations, Yangshuo is like falling into a Chinese landscape painting.

In recent years Yangshuo has become a mecca for foreign tourists, lured by the unique beauty of the surrounding countryside. The best way to explore the area is by bicycle, passing bamboo groves, orange orchards, cinnamon trees, and fields of sugar cane, peanuts, watermelons and tobacco. Moon Hill, a limestone peak marked by a moon-shaped hole, is a bike ride 10km (6 miles)

southwest of Yangshuo. A 30-minute
hike to the top provides excellent views
of the surrounding countryside.

Boat tours out of Yangshuo are
available and travel upriver to Xingping,
or downstream to Fuli. Xingping is
known for its beautiful natural scenery.
In addition to amazing views, Fuli is a
small fishing and farming village with
traditional architecture and narrow
streets. You can also hire your own
small boat for a leisurely trip down the
Li River, getting off to explore rustic
villages where fishing is still practised
with tamed cormorants.

Back in Yangshuo, cobblestoned Xi
Jie, or West Street, has a wide array of
souvenir shops to browse selling a
variety of arts and crafts. Diecui Road is
a good place for a look at a local
produce market and to mingle with
locals. For those in need of a brief break
from China, dine at one of the bar-cum-
restaurants serving Western dishes.
These places offer value for money and
are good places to get advice on the
area. Also, if you decide to stay a while,
look for schools offering classes in
Mandarin, Chinese cooking and Taichi.

✚ 2K ✉ 65km (40 miles) south of Guilin,
Guangxi Province 🚌 Buses from Guilin,
Nanning and Shenzhen 🚆 Guilin Railway
Station 🚢 Li River Cruise ($$–$$$)
✈ Guilin Airport

Best things to do

Great places to have lunch

BEIJING
Capital M ($$$)
A top-notch restaurant with excellent views over Tiananmen Square, Capital M has a central location and fine European menu.
✉ 3rd floor, 2 Qianmen Dajie ☎ (010) 6702 2727; www.capital-m-beijing.com ⏰ Daily lunch and dinner

Dali Courtyard ($$)
The Dali has a charming courtyard ambience and outstanding dishes from Yunnan in China's southwest. Dishes are designed for you by the chef. Reserve ahead.
✉ 67 Xiaojingchang Hutong ☎ (010) 8404 1430 ⏰ Daily lunch and dinner

South Silk Road (Chama Gudao) ($$)
Spicy, earthy Yunnan food is served in this popular, hip restaurant in the east of the city.
✉ 3rd Floor, Building D, Soho (Xiandaicheng), 500m (545yds) west of Guomao metro station on Dong Chang'an Jie ☎ (010) 8580 4286 ⏰ Daily 11–10:30

HONG KONG
Hutong ($$$)
Excellent, hot and spicy, north Chinese food is served here. Enjoy staggering views from a lovely, traditionally inspired interior.
✉ 28th Floor, 1 Peking Road, Tsim Sha Tsui ☎ (852) 3428 8342 ⏰ Daily lunch and dinner

Tang Court ($$$)
This elegant and famous Kowloon restaurant has an outstanding and much-loved Cantonese menu.
✉ Langham Hotel, 8 Peking Road, Tsim Sha Tsui ☎ (852) 2375 1133 ⏰ Daily lunch and dinner

MACAU
Pousada de Sao Tiago Macau ($$$)
Tasty Portuguese cuisine is served overlooking the Pearl River. This hotel is the former 17th-century fortress, Fortaleza da Barra.

✉ Avenida da Republica, Fortaleza de Sao Tiago da Barra, Macau
☎ (853) 28378 111 🕑 Daily lunch and dinner

THE PROVINCES
Chen Mapo Doufu Dian ($)
This is the home of Sichuan's famous spicy *mapo doufu* and a wide variety of other popular Sichuan snacks.

✉ 197 Xiyulong Jie, Chengdu, Sichuan ☎ (028) 8653 0162 🕑 Daily 11:30–9

Lamu's House of Tibet ($)
Warm, hospitable and ever-popular, this Lijiang restaurant has an eclectic menu embracing almost everything, but with noteworthy Tibetan and local dishes.

✉ 56 Xinyi Jie, Lijiang ☎ (0888) 511 5776
🕑 Daily 7am–late

SHANGHAI
Lynn ($$)
Mouthwatering Shanghai cuisine is served in eye-catching surroundings just off Nanjing Donglu.

✉ 99-1 Xikang Lu ☎ (021) 6247 0101 🕑 Daily 11:30–10:30

M on the Bund ($$$)
This restaurant offers excellent Western cuisine, served up with one of the most beautiful views of the Bund.

✉ 7th Floor, 20 Guangdong Lu ☎ (021) 6350 9988;
www.m-restaurantgroup.com 🕑 Daily lunch and dinner

Top activities

Exploring: from the side alleys of Pingyao to the mountains of Tibet, China is an adventure.

Trekking: explore the wildness of the Great Wall with its dramatic landscape and architecture.

Hiking: take a vigorous hike up one of China's scenic mountains – Huangshan, Taishan, Emeishan or Wutaishan.

Cycling: wherever you are, hire a bicycle and explore the real China.

Singing: grab the microphone and find out what karaoke is all about.

Shopping: hunt through China's local markets for treasures and knick-knacks.

Eating: China just wouldn't be China without its extraordinarily diverse cuisine.

Photographing: you may need an extra large memory card for your camera – China is full of photogenic surprises.

Travelling by train: take an overnight train to experience the thrill of rail travel.

Become a pilgrim: journey to some of China's holiest Buddhist and Taoist shrines to witness the religious renewal.

Best places to stay

BEIJING
Beijing Raffles ($$$)
In a tip-top setting east of the Forbidden City and Tiananmen Square, there is a rare sense of heritage hotel history here.

✉ 33 Dongchang'an Jie ☎ (010) 6526 3388; www.being.raffles.com

Peking International Youth Hostel ($)
Homely, snug and welcoming, this courtyard hostel is temptingly hidden away down a small *hutong* east of the Forbidden City.

✉ 5 Beichizi Ertiao ☎ (010) 6526 8855

HONG KONG
Peninsula Hong Kong ($$$)
Top of the line elegance can be found here, with spectacular views across Victoria Harbour from Kowloon.

✉ Salisbury Road, Tsim Sha Tsui, Kowloon ☎ (852) 2920 2888; www.peninsula.com

MACAU
Pousada de Sao Tiago ($$$)
At the tip of the Macau Peninsula with a superb view of the Pearl River Delta, the hotel is built into a Portuguese fort.

✉ Avenida de Republica, Fortaleza de Sao Tiago da Barra ☎ (853) 2837 8111; www.saotiago.com.mo

THE PROVINCES
Garden Hotel ($$)
The Garden is small enough to feel intimate but grand enough to make an impression.
✉ 59 Da Nanjie, Datong ☎ (0352) 586 5825; www.huayuanhotel.com.cn

SHANGHAI
Park Hyatt ($$$)
Sleep among the clouds above Shanghai at this luxurious Pudong hotel way above ground.
✉ 100 Century Avenue, Pudong ☎ (021) 6888 1234;
www.parkhyattshanghai.com

Peace Hotel ($$$)
A grand old-timer emerges after a long refit to once again flaunt its art deco panache and Bund-side grandeur.
✉ 20 Nanjing Donglu ☎ (021) 6321 6888; www.fairmont.com

Pudi Boutique Hotel ($$)
This gorgeous French Concession hotel has a winning sense of style, overseen by highly capable staff.
✉ 99 Yandang Road ☎ (021) 5158 5888; www.boutiquehotel.cc

Most memorable experiences

Visit a Beijing *hutong*: for Beijingers, there is perhaps nothing more emblematic of the city than its charming – but quickly vanishing – courtyard houses and narrow alleyways.

Walking along the Great Wall: choose a section of wall and go for a long hike through a dramatic landscape of mountains, gullies and ruined fortifications.

Exploring Shanghai's French Concession: Shanghai's best villa architecture, its most attractive shikumen buildings, its leafiest streets, its trendiest boutiques and some of its best cafes, restaurants and bars are all to be found in the French Concession.

Hiking around Yangshuo: hop on a bicycle or tramp around the karst landscape of Yangshuo and have your camera working overtime.

Watching the sunrise form Huangshan: take a few days to clamber up Huangshan and down again, but spend at least one night on the summit.

Visiting the Mogao Caves: the highlight of any Silk Road journey, the effigies outside Dunhuang are a reminder of the Buddhist civilization once paramount in China's northwest.

Taking the Star Ferry in Hong Kong: watch Hong Kong's Islands Central district in all its glory from the waters of Victoria Harbour.

Learning Taichi in a park: it's time to fit in with the locals, and where better than in a city park where the ancient martial art of Taichi draws adherents to practise daily.

Learning some Mandarin: now's your chance to pick up some of what is shaping up to be a major world tongue, and where better to learn?

Fully explore China's food: wherever you go in China there's one thing that will always be there – the cuisine that ranges across an amazing spectrum of flavour through the land.

Places to take the children

BEIJING
Beijing Chaoyang Theatre
The China Acrobatic Troupe offers a nightly performance including tightrope walking, plate spinning and mind-boggling gymnastics.
✉ 36 Dongsanhuanbei Lu, Chaoyang District ☎ (010) 6507 2421 🕐 Daily 5:15pm and 7:15pm (show lasts 30 min, approx) ✋ Expensive

Le Cool
Large ice-skating rink inside Beijing's classiest mall. Prada, Cartier and Louis Vitton provide distraction for the grown ups.
✉ B2, China World Shopping Mall, 1 Jianguomenwai Dajie ☎ (010) 6505 5776; www.lecoolicerink.com 🕐 Daily 10–10 ✋ Moderate

HONG KONG
Ocean Park
Includes an amusement park and a pair of giant pandas given to mark the 10th anniversary of the 1997 handover of Hong Kong.
✉ Wong Chuk Hang Road, Aberdeen, Hong Kong Island ☎ (852) 2552 0291; www.oceanpark.com.hk 🕐 Daily 10–6 ✋ Expensive

Hong Kong Disneyland
The resort has been modelled on the original 1950s Disneyland theme park in California and has virtually identical attractions.
✉ Lantau Island ☎ (852) 1 830 830; www.hongkongdisneyland.com 🕐 Daily 10–8 (approx) ✋ Expensive

Hong Kong Space Museum
Great interactive displays and a huge Space Theatre planetarium.
✉ 10 Salisbury Road, Tsim Sha Tsui, Kowloom, Hong Kong ☎ (852) 2721 0226; www.lcsd.gov.hk 🕐 Mon, Wed–Fri 1–9, Sat,Sun 10–9 ✋ Inexpensive

SHANGHAI
Science and Technology Museum
Interactive museum split into 12 main themes including Earth

Exploration, Children's Technoland, Light of Wisdom, Spectrum of Life, and Cradle of Designers.

✉ 2000 Shijidadao, Century Park, Pudong ☎ (021) 6862 2000; www.sstm.org.cn ⏰ Tue–Sun 9–5:15 ✋ Moderate

Shanghai Centre Theatre

Home to the Shanghai Acrobatics Troupe who put on a daily hour-and-a-half show featuring breathtaking feats of strength and skill.

✉ 1376 Nanjing Xilu ☎ (021) 6279 8948 ⏰ Shows begin at 7:30pm. The venue is sometimes used for music concerts. On these occasions, the acrobatics show is cancelled ✋ Expensive

Shanghai Zoo

One of China's better zoos. Unusual and rare animals include the South China tiger, Siberian tiger, red goral, ring-tailed lemur and oriental white stork. Other attractions include a roller-skating rink, and children's playground.

✉ 2381 Hongqiao Lu (near the old airport) ☎ (021) 6268 7775 ext 8000; www.shanghaizoo.cn ⏰ Daily 6:30–5 ✋ Inexpensive

Stunning views

Avenue of Stars, Hong Kong: this walkway is the best spot to drink in the spectacular city skyline of Hong Kong Island.

Beihai, Huangshan: the Beihai (North Sea) is best viewed from the Refreshing Terrace on Huangshan (➤ 122). Watch in awe as a sea of mist courses through the valley below.

Shanghai World Financial Center: put your head in the clouds on the world's highest observation deck above ground level in this fabulous tower (➤ 116).

Lake Karakul, Xinjiang: famed for its hypnotizing hues, Lake Karakul – close to the China–Pakistan border – is a dreamy vista of teardrop-blue water and snow-dipped mountain peaks.

Pingyao at night: China's most appealing ancient walled town (➤ 99) is beautifully hung with red lanterns, steeped in atmosphere and old China charm.

Qinghai–Tibet Railway: this remarkable railway journey features a host of spectacular views. Among the best is the look-out from the 5,072m-high (16,636ft) Tanggula Pass, the gateway to Tibet.

Tiananmen Square by night, Beijing: Tiananmen Square (➤ 83) takes on a completely different feel at night when the crowds thin out and the buildings are lit with thousands of golden bulbs.

Xingping, Guilin: sailing north on the Li River from Yangshuo, meander past bamboo groves and commorant fishermen before reaching Xingping (➤ 55) and the famous sugarloaf mountains.

The Great Wall: the wall north of Beijing undulates through some stunning mountainous terrain, where each season brings its own distinctive hue.

Exploring

China has a rich history, unique culture and an astonishing level of geographic diversity, but it's the sheer energy of the country that grips you. This is a land where high-rises sprout as quickly as green vegetables, and it's breathtaking to behold.

In a country of around 1.3 billion people, China's ceaseless hustle and bustle is one of its great marvels. Step out into the city at night and your senses will be assailed: smells from whirring extractor fans, music from shops that never seem to close, bright lights from overhanging street signs.

Meanwhile China's rural residents carry on serenely. From the lonely Inner Mongolian grasslands in the north, to the lush Yunnanese jungles in the south; the majestic snow peaks of Tibet out west to the waterway-cut eastern plains, the Chinese countryside reveals a quite different face of this remarkable country.

Beijing and Northern China

One of China's ancient capitals, Beijing has history in spades, coupled with a bravura modernity and a fine underground system. The order and symmetry of the old districts are offset by some daring architecture while locals are among the most affable in the Middle Kingdom.

Beijing's climate swings from scorching, sweaty summers to bone-chilling, dry winters. Unusually for a capital, Beijing lies on flat terrain close to neither river nor sea. Unconstrained by natural obstructions, the city has grown into a sprawling, bustling metropolis.

Northeast of Bejing ranges former Manchuria, homeland of the Manchu who ruled China for 250 years. Famed for its rugged

landscapes and brutal winters, Russian, Japanese and Korean influences find reflection in the region's cuisine, architecture and people. The winter highlight is the annual Harbin Ice Lantern Festival, drawing visitors from across China in January and February. Inner Mongolia is famed for its stunning grassland scenery.

BEIJING

It was not until Kublai Khan established the Yuan Dynasty in the 13th century that Beijing, then called Dadu, or Great Capital, became the capital of all of China for the first time. In 1368, the Chinese changed the name to Beiping, or "northern peace". In the Ming Dynasty, Emperor Yongle, known as the architect of Beijing, began a massive rebuilding of the city, including the Temple of Heaven and the Imperial Palace, a project that took 14 years to complete. To protect the city, a massive wall, complete with looming watchtowers, was erected. After the Manchus overthrew the Ming Dynasty in 1644, they expanded the Forbidden City and built several pleasure palaces on the outskirts.

Beijing remained the imperial capital under the Qing, though the Nationalists set up their capital in Nanjing in the 1920s and moved to Chongqing during the war with Japan (1937–1945). Beijing was

restored to top spot in 1949 when the Red Army claimed victory in the civil war against the Nationalists. The city changed dramatically over the subsequent five decades, with the old city wall being torn down in the 1950s.

Beijing's transformation went into overdrive after it won the chance to host the 2008 Olympic Games. The result has been a massively expanded underground system, stunning new architecture and a newfound sense of

purpose and pride. The cost was also massive: many old *hutong* (lanes), courtyard residences and much of the historical fabric and logic of the city has been irreparably damaged or destroyed. Rich seams of history survive in Beijing, however, although the authorities face the challenge of balancing development with thoughtful preservation of the city's heritage.

✚ 4D

Baiyunguan (White Cloud Temple)

This is one of the major Taoist temples in China, and the head quarters of the China Taoist Association. The first Taoist monastery was erected here in the eighth century, but the present structure underwent major renovations in 1956 and 1981. The monastery conducts traditional ceremonies and is regularly crowded with followers and tourists on holy days. Temple decorations contain many religious symbols, including Lingzhi fungus and storks.

✚ *Beijing 2d* ✉ 6 Baiyunguan Jie, Xibianmenwai, Xuanwu District ☎ (010) 6346 3531 🕐 Daily 8:30–4 💵 Inexpensive 🚇 Nanlishilu 🚌 46, 48, 114, 308

Beihai Gongyuan (Beihai Park)

Beihai Park was once the pleasure palace for emperors of the Liao, Jin, Yuan, Ming and Qing dynasties.

The most important structure here is the Hall of Receiving Light, which is home to a 5m-high (16ft) white jade Buddha said to have been a gift from Burma to the Empress Dowager Cixi. This is where emperors rested when on their way to the western suburbs.

Qionghua Island, in Lake Beihai, is the location of the White Dagoba and the Pavilion of Benevolent Voice, from where there are excellent views of the surrounding lakes.

✠ *Beijing 5b* ✉ Wenjin Jie, Xicheng District ☎ (010) 6403 1102
🕐 Nov–May daily 6:30pm–8pm; Jun–Oct 6am–10pm 🖐 Inexpensive
🚌 5, 101, 103, 109. To south gate: 13, 42, 105, 107, 111, 118

Gugong (Forbidden City)
Best places to see, ➤ 42–43

Guguang Xiangtai (Ancient Observatory)
The Chinese have placed great importance on astronomy since ancient times, with dynasties building observatories in their capitals so that astronomers could produce the official calendar that regulated the agricultural year and sacred ceremonies. Kublai Khan established an observatory just north of here during the Yuan Dynasty. The Ming court built the present observatory at this watchtower in 1442, and it remained in use until 1929. The original Ming and Qing instruments are displayed outside on the second level terrace.

➕ *Beijing 8d* ✉ 2 Dongbiaobei Hutong, Chaoyang District
☎ (010) 6524 2202 🕐 Tue–Sun 9–11:30, 1–4
🍽 Inexpensive 🚇 Jianguomen 🚌 1, 4, 8, 9, 20, 43, 44, 57

Guojia Dajuyuan (National Centre for the Performing Arts)
A metallic blob just west of the Great Hall of the People, Beijing's futuristic theatre looks like an apparition from a distant century. After admiring the reflective exterior and dramatic design that strongly contrasts with surrounding architecture, pop in to admire the interior and its three main halls.

➕ *Beijing 5d* ✉ Xichang'an Jie
🕐 Tue–Fri 1:30–5, Sat–Sun 9:30–5
🚇 Tian'anmen Xi

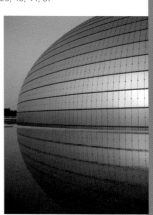

Jingshan Gongyuan (Prospect Hill Park)

Jingshan Park, which dates back to the Yuan Dynasty, was once the private playground of the imperial family. When the moat was dug for the Forbidden City, the excavated earth was used to create five hills north of the Imperial Palace. The Ten Thousand Spring Pavilion at the top of the central peak provides a stunning panoramic view of the gold and russet roofscape of the Forbidden City and Beihai Park.

✚ *Beijing 5b* ✉ Jingshan Park, north of the Forbidden City ☎ (010) 6404 4071 🕐 Apr–Sep daily 6–8:30; Oct–Mar 7–8 💲 Inexpensive 🚌 5, 111, 124, 210, 810

Kong Miao (Confucius Temple)

Confucius is considered the most important thinker in Chinese history, and his teachings were taken as the orthodox school of thought from the Han to the Qing Dynasty. First built in 1287, the temple underwent a major renovation in 1784. The quiet courtyard is lined by cypress and pine trees, and on the two sides of the yard is a collection of 188 stelae, bearing the names and birthplaces of the successful candidates in the imperial service exams from 1416–1904.

➕ *Beijing 7a* ✉ 13 Guozijian Jie, Dongcheng District ☎ (010) 8401 1977
🕐 8:30–5 ✋ Inexpensive
🚇 Yonghegong 🚌 13, 116, 117, 684

Mao Zhuxi Jiniantang (Chairman Mao Mausoleum)

After Chairman Mao Zedong died in 1976, the party ignored his wish to be cremated and ordered that his body be embalmed. Within one year of Chairman Mao's death, the

mausoleum was built at the southern end of Tiananmen Square, and Mao's body was placed in a crystal coffin draped with the red flag of the Communist Party. The coffin, located in the Hall of Mourning, is raised from its underground refrigeration unit each morning. After queuing, visitors are briskly whisked past the

embalmed Mao, hats in hand.

➕ *Beijing 5d* ✉ Tiananmen Square ☎ (010) 6513 2277
🕐 Tue–Sun 8–12 ✋ Inexpensive 🚇 Tiananmen Xi, Tiananmen Dong, Qianmen 🚌 1, 2, 4, 5, 9, 10, 17, 22, 44, 47, 48, 53, 59, 110, 116

Nanluogu Xiang

Beijing's most entertaining and fun-filled alleyway, 786m (860yds) long Nanluogu Xiang's current guise has been 10 years in the making. Some of the city's most historic *hutong* feed off from either flank, while Nanluogu Xiang itself is a long strip of hole-in-the-wall shops, micro-bars, restaurants and courtyard hotels. This is one of the best alleys to be based around and a soon-to-open underground stop will make access particularly easy, although the improved accessibility promises to add to the shopping, dining and sightseeing scrums.

A short walk west of Nanluogu Xiang are the Drum and Bell Towers and the lakes of Qianhai and Houhai.

✚ *Beijing 6a* ✉ Dongcheng District 🚌 13, 42, 118

Qianmen

Entry to the Forbidden City was controlled by a series of nine gates. Qianmen was the main point of transit between the northern Tartar district and the southern Chinese district of Beijing.

The gate was built during the 15th century. The Jianlou is just south of Qianmen, and the two gates were originally joined. At the winter solstice the emperor passed through this gate to pray at the Temple of Heaven.

Qianmen Dajie, running south of the gate, has been recently restored into a pedestrians-only Qing-style street with trams, designer shops and restaurants, while the Dashilar shopping street runs off to the west.

✚ *Beijing 5e* ✉ South side of Mao Memorial Hall ☎ (010) 6522 9386 🕐 Tue–Sun 8:30–4 🎫 Inexpensive 🚇 Qianmen 🚌 5, 17, 20, 22, 48, 59

Shisan Ling (Ming Tombs)

Thirteen of the 16 Ming emperors are buried at the Ming Tombs, along with their wives. However, only three of those tombs are open to members of the public. Changling, the burial site of the third Ming emperor, Yongle, is considered the most important. It is said that 16 concubines were buried alive with the emperor, a practice that was abandoned later in the Ming Dynasty. Dingling, the tomb of Emperor Wanli, took six years to complete, and Wanli gave a party in his own funeral chamber to mark its completion. The coffins of the emperor and his two empresses and more than 3,000 artefacts are on display in the tomb and two small museums. The Ming tombs are approached by the Sacred Way, an avenue leading to the tombs which is lined with an honour guard of 12 pairs of statues, each carved from a single stone.

➕ 4D ✉ Changping County, Tianshoushannan Lu ☎ (010) 6076 1888
🕐 Apr–Oct daily 8–5:30; Nov–Mar 8:30–5 🖐 Moderate 🚌 Direct tour bus from Qianmen or public bus 345 to Changping, then bus 314 to the tombs

Shoudu Bowuguan (Capital Museum)

This stunningly good-looking museum is perhaps the best in town (at least until the China National Museum next to Tiananmen Square reopens), with excellent displays of ancient Chinese porcelain, Buddhist statues, bronzes, art work and more in a spacious, well-designed building. Similar in range and exhibits to the Shanghai Museum (➤ 117), this is very much the kind of museum Beijing has needed for a long time and is easily reached by taking the metro to the Muxidi stop.

www.capitalmuseum.org.cn

➕ *Beijing* 1f ✉ 16 Fuxingmenwai Dajie ☎ (010) 6337 0491 🕐 Tue–Sun 9–5 🖐 Inexpensive 🚇 Muxidi

Tai Miao (Supreme Temple)

Situated within the tediously named Workers' Cultural Palace is the simply magnificent Supreme Temple, where the emperor came to worship. With its harmoniously arranged halls, the temple is an oasis of quiet and charm, right on the edge of the Forbidden City. Enveloping the temple is an equally tranquil and well-ordered park which borders the palace moat – the perfect place for taking a seat after wandering around the palace grounds.

✚ *Beijing* 6d ✉ Dongchang'an Dajie ⏲ Daily 6:30am–7pm ✋ Inexpensive
🚇 Tian'anmen Dong

Tiananmen Guangchang (Tiananmen Square)

Tiananmen Square is one of the largest public squares in the world, covering 100ha (247 acres). A public gathering place during the Ming and Qing dynasties, buildings stood on the two sides of a central path leading to the entrance of the Forbidden City. With the Forbidden City, the square is positioned at the heart of Beijing. University students came here to protest Japanese demands on China in 1919, and it was from the rostrum of the Gate of Heavenly Peace that Chairman Mao announced the establishment of the People's Republic of China in 1949. Red Guards held huge rallies in the square during the Cultural Revolution (1966–1976), and a million people gathered here in 1976 to mourn the passing of Communist leader Zhou Enlai. In 1989, the square was the site of massive anti-government student demonstrations. Monuments of note are the Mausoleum of Chairman Mao (► 79), the gates of Qianmen (► 80) in the south, and the Great Hall of the People on the west side, where China's parliament, the National People's Congress, sits. Opposite the latter is the National Museum of China, undergoing renovation and due to reopen in 2011.

🚇 *Beijing 5d* ✉ Centre of Beijing City 🚊 Tiananmen Xi, Tiananmen Dong, Qianmen 🚌 2, 4, 5, 9, 10, 17, 22, 44, 47, 48, 53, 59, 110, 116

Tiantan (Temple Of Heaven)

In its setting within a huge park, the Temple of Heaven is China's best example of Imperial temple architecture. Construction began in 1406 during the reign of Yongle and took 14 years to complete. There are three main buildings where the emperor went during the winter solstice to offer prayers and sacrifices for a good harvest. The emperor spent the night preceding the ceremony fasting in the Hall of Abstinence. The Hall of Prayer for Good Harvests stands 39m (128ft) tall and is supported by 28 wooden pillars topped by three conical roofs. The last person to use the hall was president Yuan Shikai, of the newly established republic, who had imperial ambitions and who offered imperial sacrifices on the winter solstice in 1914. The Hall of the Imperial Vault of Heaven, located in the centre, stored ceremonial tablets used in rituals. Echo Wall, a circular brick wall surrounding the Imperial Vault, has the acoustical ability to enable two people standing at opposite points to hear each other whisper. The circular terraces of the Round Altar, to the south, are where the emperor offered sacrifices and prayed.

✛ *Beijing 6f* ✉ Tiantandong Lu, Chongwen District ☎ (010) 6702 8866 ⏰ Park: daily 6–9. Temple buildings: Apr–Oct daily 8–6; Nov–Mar 8–5 (last ticket sold 90 min before closing) ✋ Moderate 🚇 Tiantandongmen 🚌 2, 15, 16, 17, 20, 35, 36, 106, 110, 116 ❓ Audio tour available

Wuta Si (Five Pagoda Temple)

This Indian-style temple was built in the 15th century during the reign of Yongle. The temple has five pagodas, each decorated with detailed Buddhist bas-reliefs. The temple was looted by Anglo-French troops following the Second Opium War in 1860 and by Western soldiers during the Boxer Rebellion in 1900.

✛ *Beijing 1a* ✉ 24 Wutasicun, Haidian ☎ (010) 6217 3836 ⏰ Tue–Sun 9–4 ✋ Inexpensive (free Wed) 🚇 Xizhimen 🚌 4, 5, 105, 107, 111, 114

Xuanwumen Tang (Southern Cathedral)

The Southern Cathedral, also known as the Cathedral of the
Immaculate Conception, is the oldest Catholic church in Beijing.
It was first erected in the middle of the 16th century by Matteo
Ricci, an Italian Jesuit missionary who arrived in China in 1583 and
received permission to live in Beijing in 1601 after impressing
Emperor Wanli with his knowledge of maths and science. The
cathedral was rebuilt in 1657, and a stone tablet erected at the
time still stands in the yard, inscribed with the words "Cathedral
Built on Imperial Order". The present structure dates back to 1904.

✚ *Beijing 4d* ✉ 141 Qianmenxi Dajie, Xuanwu District ☎ (010) 6603 7139
⏰ Services in Latin, Mon–Sat 6:30am, Sun 6:30, 7:30 and 8:30am. Service in
English, Sun 10am, 4pm 🚇 Xuanwumen 🚌 5, 15, 25, 44, 45, 48, 49

Xu Beihong Bowuguan (Xu Beihong Museum)

One of the most famous modern Chinese painters, Xu Beihong (1895–1953) is especially known for his vivid paintings of galloping horses. The museum has seven rooms, five dedicated to displaying Xu's sketches and paintings and offering an introduction to his life and work. His painting studio and sitting room are displayed here, with his brushes and paints on a table as if ready for use. An unfinished oil painting stands on an easel, as it did when he died. The museum also includes 1,200 paintings by other famous Chinese painters, 10,000 rare books, illustrations and stone rubbings.

➕ *Beijing 4a* ✉ 53 Xinjiekoubei Dajie, Xicheng District ☎ (010) 6227 6936 ⏰ Tue–Sun 9–4:30 💷 Inexpensive 🚇 Jishuitan 🚌 22, 27, 38, 44, 47

Yiheyuan (Summer Palace)

This complex of buildings and gardens dates back 800 years when the first emperor of the Jin Dynasty built the Gold Mountain Palace at the site now known as Longevity Hill. Succeeding dynasties expanded the complex. The imperial court would come here in the summer to get away from the heat of Beijing. The palace was damaged by Anglo-French troops in 1860 during the Second Opium War, and was burned down by Western soldiers in retaliation for the Boxer Rebellion in 1900, but it was restored in 1903. The 700m (763yds) Long Corridor, a long covered wooden walkway that runs across the south shore of the lake, is decorated with auspicious symbols and landscape paintings on the beams. Emperor Guangxu and Empress Dowager Cixi received ministers in the Hall of Benevolent

Longevity. The Hall of Jade Ripples is where Cixi put Guangxu under house arrest in 1898 after the young emperor attempted to carry out far-reaching reforms. He remained here until his death in 1908, allegedly poisoned by Cixi, who died one day later. At the west end of the lake is the famous marble boat built by Cixi with money intended for creating a modern Chinese navy.

➕ *Beijing 1a (off map)* ✉ Yiheyuan, northwest of Haidian District ☎ (010) 6288 1144 🕐 Apr–Oct daily 6:30–6; Nov–Mar 7–5 ✋ Moderate 🚇 Xiyuan 🚌 303, 304, 332, 333, 346, 726, 801, 808, 904

Yonghe Gong (Lama Temple)

After Qing Emperor Yongzheng ascended the throne in 1723, his former palace, built in 1694, was converted into a Lamaist temple. Lamaism, the popular name for Tibetan Buddhism, was practised by the Manchu rulers during the Qing Dynasty. During the reign of Qianlong the temple became a centre of learning for the Yellow Hat sect of Tibetan Buddhism, and exercised considerable religious and political influence. At its peak, some 1,500 Tibetan, Mongol and Chinese Lamas lived here. The temple was shut down during the Cultural Revolution, but was saved from destruction by Zhou Enlai. The temple is a complex of five halls and courtyards.

➕ *Beijing 7a* ✉ 12 Yonghegong Dajie, Dongcheng District (near the northeast corner of Second Ring Road)
☎ (010) 6404 4499 ⏰ Daily 9–4 ✋ Inexpensive
🚇 Yonghegong 🚌 13, 44, 106, 107, 116

Yuanmingyuan (Old Summer Palace)

This palace, a complex of three large gardens, was built for the emperor Qianlong during the Qing Dynasty. It was seriously damaged by Anglo-French troops in 1860 after the Second Opium War, and again during the Boxer Rebellion in 1900. Little is left of it today except for some broken pillars and masonry lying scattered around, though the gardens are very pleasant. The Garden History Exhibition Hall, not far from the ruins in the northeast of the gardens, has drawings and models of the palace during better days.

➕ *Beijing 1a (off map)* ✉ 28 Qinghua Lu, Haidian District ☎ (010) 6262 8501 🕐 Daily 7–7 ✋ Inexpensive 🚇 Yuanmingyuan Park 🚌 331, 365, 375

Zhong Lou and Gu Lou (Bell and Drum Tower)

The Drum Tower was built in 1424 during the Ming Dynasty. In imperial times, 24 drums announced the night watches. The Bell Tower was erected in 1747. The bronze bell was rung daily until 1924, when the last emperor was forced to leave the Forbidden City. It is said the bell could be heard 20km (12.5 miles) away.

➕ *Beijing 5a* ✉ 9 Zhonggulou Daijie/Dianmenwai Dajie, Dongcheng District ☎ (010) 6401 2674 🕐 Daily 9–5 ✋ Inexpensive 🚇 Guloudajie 🚌 5, 58, 60, 107

Zhoukoudian

In 1929 the discovery of the first skull of Peking Man was found at this site on Dragon Bone Hill, dating back 300,000–500,000 years. The museum at Zhoukoudian introduces the Zhoukoudian culture, including displays of implements used by Peking Man. The fossils vanished during World War II and have never been recovered.

➕ *Beijing 1e (off map)* ✉ Nanfangshan, Zhoukoudian Village, Jingxi, 48km (30 miles) southwest of Beijing

a cycling tour

around Beijing

Begin at Donghuamen, the east gate of the Forbidden City. Turn left at the gate and follow the red wall of the Forbidden City, stopping along the way to listen to amateur Peking opera singers and musicians.

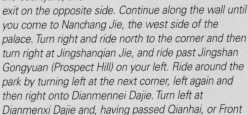

Ride to the front courtyard of the Forbidden City, cross the courtyard, and exit on the opposite side. Continue along the wall until you come to Nanchang Jie, the west side of the palace. Turn right and ride north to the corner and then turn right at Jingshanqian Jie, and ride past Jingshan Gongyuan (Prospect Hill) on your left. Ride around the park by turning left at the next corner, left again and then right onto Dianmennei Dajie. Turn left at Dianmenxi Dajie and, having passed Qianhai, or Front Lake, take the first road on your right.

On this peaceful street you'll find locals sitting beneath willow trees playing Chinese chess or doing exercises.

Cross the tiny Silver Ingot Bridge that spans a channel in the lake and turn left along Houhaibeiyan, which runs along the east side of Houhai, or the Rear Lake. From here continue on to the junction with Deshengmennei

Dajie. Turn left and cross over the bridge. You'll soon come to the Kong Yiji Restaurant (▶ 103) inside a circular whitewashed Chinese Gate.

The restaurant is named after Lu Xun's short story of the same name.

After lunch jump back onto your bicycle, turn left into the Yangfang Hutong and peddle

onwards to Liuyin Jie, on your right. Head straight down this street to Gongwangfu, the former palace of Prince Gong, younger brother of the Xianfeng Emperor (1851–1861).

Distance: 3.5km (2 miles)
Time: 2–3 hours
Start point: Donghuamen, East Gate, Forbidden City ✚ *Beijing 6c*
End point: Gongwangfu (Prince Gong's Mansion) ✚ *Beijing 5a*
Lunch: Kong Yiji Restaurant (▶ 103); Deshengmennei Dajie; tel: (010) 6618 4915

Hebei Province

CHANGCHENG (THE GREAT WALL)
Best places to see, ➤ 38–39.

CHENGDE
In 1703, Emperor Kangxi began the construction of a **Summer Palace** in Chengde, known in Chinese as the "Mountain Retreat to Escape the Heat". The palace was used by Qing emperors while on hunting trips or making military inspection tours. The palace area served as the administrative and residential quarters of the emperors. The Hall of Frugality and Calm, which is built of cedar wood, is where the emperor met with court officials, generals, foreign envoys and the heads of northern tribes. The Hall of Refreshing Mists and Waves was the royal bedroom, but also was the site of famous historical events, such as the signing of the so-called unequal treaties with the Europeans in the 19th century.

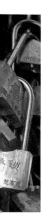

Twelve temples were built outside the palace walls, eight of them belonging to the Yellow Sect of Buddhism for the purpose of winning the support of Mongolians and Tibetans. Puning Temple is the most impressive, housing a glittering 22m (72ft) high wooden, multi-armed statue of Guanyin. The Putuozongcheng Temple is a striking reduced copy of the Potala Palace in Lhasa. The Temple of Sumeru, Happiness and Longevity is a replica of the Tashilhunpo in Shigatse, with "fish-scale" ridges on its roof and dragons.

🚹 4C ✉ 256km (159 miles) northeast of Beijing 🍴 Restaurants on Lizhengmen Dajie opposite the Summer Palace ($) 🚌 Daily from Beijing and Tianjin 🚉 Express train N211 from Beijing Station or the 2101/2105/2108 service from Beijing North Station

Imperial Summer Palace
✉ Lizhengmen Dajie 🕐 16 Apr– 14 Oct daily 7–5:30; 15 Oct–15 Apr 7–4:30
✋ Moderate

QING DONG LING (EASTERN QING TOMBS)

Five emperors, 14 empresses and 136 concubines are buried at the Eastern Qing Tombs, including Kangxi, Qianlong, Xuanfeng, Tongzhi and Empress Dowager Cixi. Emperor Shunzhi chose the site because of its good fengshui, or geomancy. The marble vault of Qianlong is the most interesting, with beautifully carved Buddhas. Cixi's tomb is also decorated with imperial motifs such as dragons and phoenixes.

🚹 4D ✉ Just before Changrui, Zunhua County, Hebei Province, 125km (77.5 miles) east of Beijing

SHANHAIGUAN

This former Ming dynasty garrison town has an impressive town wall, city gates, *hutong* and recently rebuilt temples and towers. The Great Wall meets the sea at Laolongtou while bracing hikes up the barricade can be made at Jiaoshan, north of town.

🚹 17P ✉ 290km (180 miles) east of Beijing 🚉 The D5 express from Beijing takes under two hours

Heilongjiang Province

HARBIN

Harbin, from a Manchu word meaning "where fishing nets dry", was first settled by the Manchu people in the 11th century. It remained a small hunting and fishing village until 1896, when the Russian czar and the Qing court agreed that Russia would build a railroad linking Dalian, Harbin, and the Trans-Siberian Railroad with Vladivostok. Today, the capital of Heilongjiang Province, the city retains many traces of its Russian heritage.

Some Russian Orthodox churches were seriously damaged during the Cultural Revolution, but some have been renovated. The magnificent **St Sofia's church,** built in 1907, is an excellent example of the Byzantine style and houses an exhibition on the architectural history of the city. The main part of the church is cruciform in style, capped with a green onion dome. The city's glittering Ice Lantern Festival draws in visitors from all over China, despite – or because of – the shockingly cold weather.

🚩 6A 🖂 Capital of Heilongjiang Province, northeast China 🚆 Daily express trains from Beijing ✈ Harbin Airport ❓ Ice Lantern Festival, 5 Jan–15 Feb

St Sofia's Church

🖂 88 Toulong Jie, between Zhaolin Jie and Diduan Jie 🕐 Daily 9:30–5 Inexpensive 🚌 13, 16, 23,101, 102, 103, 116

Shaanxi Province

XI'AN

Formerly Chang'an, Xi'an served as the capital of China for 1,100 years, and the treasure trove of artefacts – notably the world-famous Terracotta Warriors – are a reminder of the city's glorious past. Xi'an reached the height of its glory during the Tang Dynasty when it represented the eastern terminus of the Silk Road. It was

arguably the greatest city in the world during this era, famous for its beautiful temples, grand mosques and palaces.

Down the road from the Terracotta site is Huaqing Hot Springs, used as an Imperial resort for hundreds of years. The palace includes gardens and elaborate structures dating back to the Qing Dynasty.

Other sights in town include the Great Mosque and the Muslim Quarter's pinched backstreets, the Bell Tower, where a bronze bell struck each morning as the city gates opened, and the Drum Tower. East of Xi'an rises the sacred Taoist mountain of Huashan with its peaks and gullies infused with superstition and myth.

➕ 1F ✉ Capital of Shaanxi Province 🚌 Buses to Luoyang and Pingyao ✈ Daily from Beijing, Chengdu, Guangzhou, Shanghai ✈ Xiguan International Airport (40km/25 miles northwest of city)

ℹ Xian Railway Station; tel: (029) 668 8688

Cheng Qiang (City Walls)

Xian's city wall is regarded as the most complete of its kind in China. Recent restoration means it's now possible to walk or cycle the entire 13.7km (8.5 miles) circumference. The 12m-high (39ft) wall was built in 1374 but was raised on the foundations of a much older structure – the Imperial compound of the Tang emperors. You can scale the wall at the four compass points though most visitors chose the South Gate where you can hire a bicycle.

🕐 Apr–Oct daily 8am–8:30pm; Nov–Mar 8–7 ✋ Moderate (the wall-top tram charges 5RMB per stop or 50RMB for the entire circuit)

Da Yan Ta (Greater Wild Goose Pagoda)

Regarded by many as the symbol of the city, the Big Goose Pagoda is located in the Da Ci'en Si (Temple of Maternal Grace) and is the oldest building in Xian. The seven-storey structure was built in AD652 at the behest of legendary monk, Xuanzang, who walked his way to India in the name of Buddhist learning. About 2km (1.6 miles) northwest is Jianfu Si (Jianfu Temple) which houses the Little Goose Pagoda. At 43m (141ft), it's smaller but, being closer to the old city, the views from the top are excellent.

Da Yan Ta

✉ Yanta Lu ☎ (029) 8553 5014 🕐 Daily 8–6:30 ✋ Inexpensive 🚌 5, 19, 21 (separate tickets to enter temple and climb pagoda)

Xiao Yan Ta

✉ Youyi Xilu ☎ (029) 8781 1081 🕐 8:30–4:30 ✋ Inexpensive 🚌 21, 29, 402

Shaanxi History Museum (Shanxi Lishi Bowuguan)

One of China's top museums, showcasing the very best in Chinese history, Shaanxi History Museum has a collection of around 370,000 exhibits. Early history is covered, including Zhou dynasty bronzes, but there are particularly impressive displays from Xian's – and China's – two greatest eras, the Han and Tang dynasties, as well as four original Terracotta Warrior statues taken from close to the tomb of Qin Shi Huang.

www.sxhm.com

✉ 91 Xiaozhai Donglu

☎ (029) 8521 9422

🕐 Apr–Oct Tue–Sun
8:30–6, last admission
4:30pm; Nov–Mar
Tue–Sun 9:30–5, last
admission 4pm 💰 Free;
admission limited to 4,000
people per day 🚌 5, 14,
610, 701

The Old City

A cluster of important
landmarks lies in the
heart of old Xian. The
main prayer hall is not open to visitors but the rest of the
Daqingzhen Si (Great Mosque) can be explored. Originally built in
AD743 by Persian merchants, it was moved to Huajue Xiang in the
14th century, though the current building dates only from the 18th
century. With a traditional Chinese pagoda serving as the minaret,
the mosque melds a traditional Chinese temple layout with Persian
embellishments. Close by are **Zhong Lou and Gu Lou** (Bell and
Drum Towers) facing each other across Bell Drum Tower Square.
The bell was rung at dawn and the drum struck at dusk.

Daqingzhen Si

✉ 30 Huajue Xiang 🕐 Mar–Nov daily 8–7:30; Dec–Feb 8–5:30
💰 Inexpensive

Zhong Lou and Gu Lou

✉ Zhong Lou: Junction of Xi Dajie and Dong Dajie; Gu Lou: Beiyuanmen
🕐 Apr–Oct 8:30am–9:30pm; Nov–Mar 8:30–5:30 💰 Inexpensive

BINGMAYONG (TERRACOTTA WARRIORS)

Best places to see, ➤ 36–37.

Shanxi Province

DATONG XUANKONG SI
(HANGING TEMPLE)

The Hanging Temple has been clinging precariously to the near vertical cliff of Golden Dragon Gorge for some 14 centuries. Constructed by Taoist monks known as "Feathered Scholars", and renovated numerous times, the six main halls and other rooms are linked by a mixture of winding corridors, bridges and boardwalks. Known in Chinese as the "Monastery in Mid-Air", the temple was built in stages on pillars positioned in both natural and man-made holes found in the face of the cliff.

➕ 3D ✉ 75km (46.5 miles) southeast of Datong, Shanxi Province
☎ (0352) 832 7795 🕓 Daily 8–6 🖐 Moderate 🚌 Bus from Datong to
Hunyuan. Minibuses from Hunyuan

PINGYAO

Possibly the best-preserved ancient walled town in China, Pingyao
is a gorgeous place to spend three or four days – almost every
other courtyard house is a hotel. Once China's first banking centre,
it has history galore, from historic alleyways, to the magnificent
town walls, the Confucius Temple, the City Tower, the
Rishengcheng Financial House Museum and much more. The
nearby Shuanglin Temple is a bicycle ride away, with its fantastic
statues; the Wang Family Courtyard is a magnificent Shanxi
courtyard residence within reach of Pingyao.

➕ 2E ✉ 100km (62 miles) south of Taiyuan, Shanxi Province
🍴 Restaurants and bars along Nan Dajie and Xi Dajie ($) 🚌 Daily from
Taiyuan 🚆 Overnight from Beijing, daily from Taiyuan; ticket price: moderate

WUTAISHAN

Wutaishan, or Five Terrace Mountain, is one of China's four sacred
Buddhist mountains. Close to Inner Mongolia, Wutaishan was a
pilgrimage site for Mongolians devoted to Tibetan Buddhism. The
Tang and Ming dynasties were the most prosperous periods in
Wutaishan, when the mountain had 200 monasteries. Numbers are
way down today, but the valley village of Taihuai (where the hotels
and restaurants are) still has active temples – including the dagoba
of Tayuan Temple and the Xiantong Temple with its magnificent
Golden Hall. Two of China's oldest temple buildings, Nanchan
Temple and Foguang Temple, are a bus journey from Taihuai.
www.wutaishan.cn

➕ 3D ✉ Yangboyu Village, Taihuai Town, 240km (149 miles) northeast of
Taiyuan, Shanxi Province ☎ (0350) 654 3133 🖐 Moderate 🚌 Minibuses
from Datong (summer only) and Taiyuan. Private minibuses make trips to
various temples around Wutaishan 🚆 Train to Datong or Taiyuan

HOTELS

BEIJING
Beijing Raffles Hotel ($$$)
See page 62.

Guxiang 20 ($$$)
Attractively designed, this traditional-style hotel is set on a *hutong* near the Bell and Drum Tower.
✉ 20 Nanluogu Xiang, Dongcheng District ☎ (010) 6400 5566; www.guxiang20.com

Opposite House Hotel ($$$)
This nattily designed hotel in the Sanlitun area of east Beijing garners rave reviews across the spectrum for its stylish rooms, superb restaurants and bars.
✉ 11 Sanlitun Lu, Chaoyang District ☎ (010) 6417 6688; www.theoppositehouse.com

Park Plaza ($$$)
Just off Wangfujing Dajie, with a restrained sense of style, the Park Plaza has cheaper rooms than the next door Regent.
✉ 97 Jinbao Jie, Dongcheng District ☎ (010) 8522 1999; www.parkplaza.com

Peking International Youth Hostel ($$–$$$)
See page 62.

Red Capital Residence ($$$)
A small boutique hotel located in a traditional courtyard house. Each of the five suites has an intriguing name such as "Concubine of the East". Look for the red door with the number 9.
✉ 9 Dongsi Liutiao, Dongcheng District ☎ (010) 6402 7150; www.redcapitalclub.com.cn

Shangri-La Hotel ($$$)
Another one of China's superb string of Shangri-La hotels. Located in northwest Beijing, this place has every conceivable facility,

including its own delicatessen and shopping arcade. Well placed for the Summer Palace.

✉ 29 Zizhuyuan Lu, Haidian District ☎ (010) 6841 8002; www.shangri-la.com

St. Regis Hotel ($$$)

The St. Regis is a first-class hotel located on the grounds of the historic Beijing International Club and close to Beijing's Jianguomenwai business district. Facilities include a spa and indoor heated pool.

✉ 21 Jianguomenwai Dajie, Chaoyang District ☎ (010) 6460 6688; www.stregis.com

CHENGDE
Mountain Villa Hotel ($)

Perfectly located for the Imperial Summer Palace. The hotel has six restaurants, a business centre and a variety of suites and rooms to suit all tastes.

✉ 11 Lizhengmen Lu ☎ (0314) 209 1188; www.hemvhotel.com

DATONG
Garden Hotel ($$)

See page 63.

HARBIN
Holiday Inn ($–$$)

Close to Harbin's historic Daoliqu area and St Sophia's Church. Facilities include a gym, sauna and massage rooms.

✉ 90 Jingwei Jie ☎ (0451) 8422 6666

PINGYAO
Harmony Guesthouse ($)

Fantastic and ever-popular, this place is operated by an English-speaking couple. The Harmony has delightful rooms and courtyard charms. The owners can pick up guests from the train station and purchase tickets.

✉ 165 Nan Dajie ☎ (0354) 568 4952; www.py-harmony.com

WUTAISHAN
Qixiange Binguan ($$)
Qixiange Binguan offers the best accommodation at the foot of
the mountain. The hotel is in a peaceful setting close to nature.
✉ 2.5km (1.5 miles) south of Taihuai, near Nanshan Monastery ☎ (0350)
654 2400

Wufeng Binguan ($)
This four-star hotel, located beside the Longquan Temple within the
scenic area, is the best hotel in Wutaishan and is well priced.
✉ Taihuai Town ☎ (0350) 644 8988; www.5f-hotel.com

XI'AN
Hyatt Regency Xi'an (Xian Kaiyue Fandian) ($$$)
Situated within the walls of the old city. The grand interior and the
high standards of service make this hotel a delight.
✉ 158 Dong Dajie ☎ (029) 8769 1234; www.xian.regency.hyatt.com

RESTAURANTS

BEIJING
Bookworm ($)
A great cafe, meeting place and first-rate bookshop, this is the
venue of the annual Beijing International Literary Festival in March.
✉ Building 4 Nansanlitun Lu ☎ (010) 6586 9507 🕐 Daily 9am–1am

Café Sambal ($)
Cooking up Malaysian dishes in a traditional *hutong*, this popular
restaurant has a charming courtyard setting and authentic menu.
✉ 43 Doufuchi Hutong ☎ (010) 6400 4875 🕐 Daily lunch and dinner

Capital M ($$$)
See page 58.

Dadong Roast Duck Restaurant ($$)
Judged by many to be the best duck in town, this place offers a
less fatty bird compared with other duck restaurants; book ahead.
✉ Building 3, Tuanjie Beikou ☎ (010) 6582 2892 🕐 Daily lunch and dinner

Dali Courtyard ($$)
See page 58.

Dongbeiren ($)
Lively and welcoming, this Manchurian Chinese restaurant has a hearty, no-fuss and tasty menu.

✉ 1 Xinzhong Jie ☎ (010) 6415 2855 🕐 Daily lunch and dinner

Donglaishun ($$)
Muslim-style hot pot is the speciality here. Cook meat and vegetables in a boiling broth at your own table, and then dunk the food into a special sauce.

✉ 5th Floor, Xindong'an Plaza, Wangfujing Dajie ☎ (010) 6528 0932
🕐 Daily lunch and dinner

Element Fresh ($)
A big, big hit for years in Shanghai, Element Fresh has brought its cool lines and crisp sandwiches to Beijing.

✉ Building 8, The Village, Sanlitun Lu ☎ (010) 6417 1318 🕐 Mon–Fri 11–11, Sat–Sun 8am–11pm

Kong Yiji ($$)
This tastefully designed restaurant, in a lovely setting beside Houhai lake, specializes in Zhejiang cuisine. Try *huixiangdou* (lima beans) or *choudoufu* (smelly bean curd), with Shaoxing wine.

✉ 2 Dongming Hutong, Houhai South Bank, Deshengmennei Dajie, Xicheng district ☎ (010) 6618 4915 🕐 Daily lunch and dinner

Quan Ju De ($$)
No one does Peking duck better than this famous – if slightly expensive – old restaurant. The bird is wheeled to the table and its crispy skin expertly sliced off in front of you.

✉ 32 Qianmen Dajie, Chongwen district ☎ (010) 6511 2418
🕐 Daily lunch and dinner

South Silk Road (Chama Gudao) ($$)
See page 58.

EXPLORING

DATONG
Yonghe Meishicheng Restaurant ($$)
This slightly (for Datong) classy restaurant offers a wide variety of
Chinese dishes. A picture menu makes ordering easier.

✉ 3 Yingbin Donglu ☎ (0352) 510 3008 🕐 Lunch, dinner

HARBIN
Ding Ding Xiang ($)
Sort out the cold of a Harbin winter with one of the fantastic hot
pots here. It's a tasty, fun and social way to dine.

✉ 58 Jingwei Jie 🕐 Daily 10:30am–11pm

PINGYAO
Yunjingcheng Binguan ($$–$$$)
Sample Shanxi dishes including fried buns stuffed with *jianbao*
(meat), or the local noodles in this courtyard restaurant and hotel.

✉ Mingqing Dajie, opposite the Xietongqing Museum ☎ (0354) 568 0944;
www.pibc.com 🕐 Lunch, dinner

XI'AN
Laosun Jia Restaurant ($$)
This well-known restaurant specializes in Muslim and Xi'an dishes,
including *yangrou paomo* (bread and lamb cooked in broth).

✉ 364 Dongda Jie ☎ (029) 8240 3205 🕐 Lunch, Dinner

SHOPPING

BEIJING
ARTS AND CRAFTS
798 Art District
The sprawling art district is excellent for stocking up on trendy
clothes, paintings, sculpture, old photographs and art works.

✉ 2 and 4 Jiuxianqiao Lu, Chaoyang District ☎ (010) 6438 4862
🕐 Daily 10–6

Hongqiao Market
Also known as the Pearl Market, in addition to fresh water pearls
and other jewellery, Hongqiao also sells handicrafts.

✉ 46 Tiantan Donglu (close to the east gate of the Temple of Heaven), Chongwen District, Beijing ☎ (010) 6713 3354

Liulichang
Come here for curio and book shops in a remodelled Qing Dynasty street.
✉ One block south and east of the Xuanwumen subway station, Beijing

Panjiayuan Folk Culture Market
An amazing collection of items are sold in this indoor market: everything from genuine antiques to copies: handicrafts, paintings, porcelain, religious art and minority crafts are just some of the artefacts on offer. The market has an outdoor section on Saturdays and Sundays which opens around sunrise. Go early.
✉ Panjiayuan Lu, just inside the east third ring road, close to the Panjiayuan Bridge, Beijing ☎ (010) 6775 2405

Ruifuxiang Silk and Fabric Store
Find raw silk in a dazzling array of colours, textures and patterns. The store has been in business for more than a century and used to serve Qing royalty.
✉ 5 Dazhalan Jie, Xuanwu district, Beijing ☎ (010) 6303 5313
🕐 Daily 9–10

ART GALLERIES
Courtyard Gallery
Paintings and sculptures by well-known contemporary Chinese artists are displayed in the modern courtyard house which is home to the gallery.
✉ 95 Donghuamen Dajie, Chaoyang District, Beijing ☎ (010) 6526 8883

BOOKS AND MUSIC
Foreign Languages Bookstore
You will find an excellent range of English books on the top floor with seats for slow browsing. There's also a great selection of childrens' books.
✉ 235 Wangfujing Dajie ☎ (010) 6512 6911 🕐 Daily 9:30–9:30

SHOPS, MALLS AND DEPARTMENT STORES

Oriental Plaza

This is Beijing's biggest shopping mall, with many designer names.

✉ 1 Dong Chang'an Jie, Beijing ☎ (010) 8518 6363; www.orientalplaza.com
🕐 Daily 9:30am–10pm

The Place

The Place is one of Beijing's latest and most up-to-date malls.

✉ 9A Guanghua Lu ☎ (010) 8595 1755 🕐 Daily 10–10

Sanlitun Yashow Clothing Market

Immense fun and a real cornucopia of bargains galore (but haggle like crazy) in a multi-storey setting.

✉ 58 Gongrentiyuchang Beilu ☎ (010) 6416 8945 🕐 Daily 10–9

Silk Street

There are loads of floors selling silk, shoes, suitcases and traditional Chinese tailors. This is a good place for a foot massage.

✉ Corner of Jianguomenwai Dajie and Dongdaqiao Lu 🕐 Daily 9–9

The Village

This new high-profile and trendy shopping mall is right at the very heart of Sanlitun, with all the top names making an appearance including the world's largest Adidas store.

✉ 19 Sanlitun Lu 🕐 Daily 10–10

SHOPPING STREETS

Qianmen Dajie and Dazhalan

Qianmen Dajie was renovated in 2008 into a pedestrian shopping street, with designer shops and tourist trams. The historic shopping street of Dazhalan has also been restored.

Wangfujing Dajie, Beijing

Although this old street, once Beijing's premier shopping area, has been renovated, with much of it taken up by new shopping malls, it still has a large selection of interesting small and old shops. It's a great place for a stroll and window-shopping.

ENTERTAINMENT

ARTS

Laoshe Teahouse
Laoshe Teahouse features opera, magic tricks and acrobatic displays. The opera shows are usually enlivened with appropriate comedy routines.

✉ 3 Qianmenxi Dajie, Chongwen District, Beijing ☎ (010) 6303 6830; www.laosheteahouse.com 🕐 Daily 7:40 and 9:20pm

Liyuan Theatre
Beijing's most well-known theatre for a Western audience has screens alongside the stage for helpful English translations.

✉ Qianmen Hotel, 175 Yongan Lu, Xuanwu District, Beijing ☎ (010) 6301 6688 ext 8860 🕐 Daily 7:30–8:40pm

Sanwei Bookstore
Traditional Chinese music is performed by some of Beijing's best classical musicians in a rustic teashop. Reservations are recommended.

✉ 60 Fuxingmennei Dajie, Xicheng District, Beijing ☎ (010) 6601 3204 🕐 Sat 8:30–10:30pm

China Puppet Theatre
The ancient art of Chinese shadow and hand puppetry is kept alive here at the China Puppet Art Theatre. Troupes from all over China regularly visit for shows. Performances are at weekends only.

✉ 1 Anhuaxili, Chaoyang District, Beijing ☎ (010) 6425 4847; www.puppetchina.com (in Chinese) 🕐 Sat–Sun 10:30am and 1:30pm

NIGHTLIFE

Banana
A loud and raucous nightclub on the first floor, this establishment also has a much quieter chill-out area above. Banana regularly attracts a string of international DJs. There is a cover charge of 20 to 30 RMB.

✉ Scietch Hotel, 22 Jianguomenwai Dajie, Chaoyang District, Beijing ☎ (010) 6528 3636 🕐 Daily 8:30pm–4am

Bed Bar

Bed bar is very cool, comfortable and an excellent hangout at the end of the day with beds provided for visitors fed up with walking around town.

✉ 17 Zhangwang Hutong, Beijing ☎ (010) 8400 1554 🕓 Mon–Tue 4pm–late, Wed–Sun noon–late

Drum & Bell

You can't beat this bar's location, with an adorable perch between the Drum and Bell Towers. Inside, the bar is cosy and upstairs is a fabulous roof terrace with views over the Beijing *hutong* rooftops.

✉ 41 Zhonglouwan Hutong, Beijing ☎ (010) 8403 3600 🕓 Daily 1pm–2am

Passby Bar

A fantastic courtyard bar, Passby serves great food and has an excellent Nanluogu Xiang location.

✉ 108 Nanluogu Xiang, Dongcheng District, Beijing ☎ (010) 8403 8004 🕓 Daily 9:30am–2am

SPORT

Beijing International Golf Club (Ming Tombs Golf Course)

About one hour from the centre of Beijing, this is considered to be the capital's best course.

✉ North of Shisanling Reservoir, Changping County ☎ (010) 6076 2288

China World Fitness Centre

Pay a visit to enjoy the squash courts, indoor tennis courts and the swimming pool.

✉ China World Trade Centre, 1 Jianguomenwai Dajie, Chaoyang District, Beijing ☎ (010) 6505 2266 🕓 Daily 6am–11pm

Nanshan Ski Resort

The largest ski resort in the Beijing area with some of the most advanced facilities in the country. The 18 runs cater for all abilities, though the snow is man-made.

✉ Shengshuitou Village, Miyun County, Beijing ☎ (010) 8909 1909; www.nanshanski.com

Shanghai and Eastern China

Eastern China is home to some of China's wealthiest and best-looking cities. Foremost among them is Shanghai, a city swaggering audaciously into the future. Then there's the towering Ming city walls and epic story of Nanjing and the lush water towns around Suzhou in Jiangsu province, where age-old China charm holds sway. Hangzhou in Zhejiang province is famed for its splendid West Lake and easy-going rhythms, while the Buddhist island of Putuoshan offshore adds sacred allure. Rising up gloriously in the south of Anhui province is Huangshan, the iconic mountain of mists.

□ Shanghai

It may have decayed over the centuries, but the Grand Canal – segments of which date back 2,500 years – carves a path to the north of China. Confucius is still venerated in his Shandong birthplace, Qufu, and Taishan, the holiest of Taoist mountains, attracts bands of visitors seeking to tap into its spiritual energies and commune with the splendid views.

SHANGHAI

China's most cosmopolitan and densely populated city, Shanghai's bustling streets are today packed with life. Crowds rush around, beeping taxis fight for space, gleaming new department stores overflow with goods, while boutique hotels, dazzling cocktail bars and chic restaurants deliver cosmopolitan élan. Shanghai is typified by the Bund and the well-bred poise of its French Concession, but its signature image today is Lujiazui, that section of Pudong embedded with skyscrapers and iconic towers across the Huangpu River.

In Chinese history terms, Shanghai is a relatively young city. Prior to the Treaty of Nanjing and the opening of the five treaty ports in 1842, it was a humble fishing village near the mouth of the Yangtze River. This all changed, however, when British, French and American settlers teamed up with enterprising Chinese merchants to turn Shanghai into a cosmopolitan city and centre of commerce. During the city's 1920s and 1930s heyday, successful

entrepreneurs and celebrities from around the world – such as the playwright Noel Coward and actor Charlie Chaplin – mixed it up in the local hotels, restaurants and clubs.

Time stood still for three decades following liberation in 1949, as the communist leadership warily viewed the city's decadent past and reputation for freewheeling capitalism. When China opened its doors to the outside world in the late 1970s, Shanghai was a pale shadow of its past self. The Shanghainese, who pride themselves in being the most savvy and enterprising people in China, lost no time in seeking to revive the city's glory. Shanghai underwent a massive transformation, seemingly building overnight state-of-the-art skyscrapers and modern expressways to speed traffic around the bustling city. China's first stock exchange opened here in 1990, and in Pudong, the land east of the Huangpu River, a modern economic zone and thriving commercial centre has risen from land that was previously used for farming little more than 20 years ago.

✚ 6G

Faguo Zujie (French Concession)

Characterized by French 1920s villas, art deco apartment blocks, shikumen architecture, tree-lined backstreets, chic cafes, delicatessens, top-name restaurants, swish boutiques, shopping malls, historic churches and charming parks, the French Concession is Shanghai's most stylish quarter. As a foreign concession following the Treaty of Nanking in 1842, the French Concession had its own buses and trams, electricity, judicial system and traffic regulations. The heart of the old concession was Avenue Joffre, today's Huaihai Lu, still the city's premier draw for shoppers. For a breather, take a seat in Fuxing Park, built by the French in Parisian style.
✉ Huaihai Lu Zhonglu 🚇 South Huangpi Road, South Shanxi Road, Changshu Road 🚌 911, 42

Huangpu Jiang (Huangpu River Tour)

The Huangpu River, 110km (68 miles) long, runs from Lake Taihu and empties into the Yangtze River some 28km (17 miles) downstream from the centre of Shanghai. In the past, large ships would enter the Yangtze, make the short journey along the deep channel of the Huangpu and unload their cargo at the wharves along the Bund. The goods were then transported by

barges along Suzhou Creek and networks of canals for distribution throughout China.

The Huangpu boat tours leave from the southern end of the Bund.

✉ 239 Zhongshan Dong Erlu ☎ (021) 6374 4461; www.pujiangyoulan.com 🕓 Daily 9:30–9:30, sailings every 30 min 🖐 Moderate 🚇 Nanjing Donglu

Nanjing Lu (Nanjing Road)

Shanghai's most famous street, Nanjing Lu, was once known as the Dama Lu, or "Great Horse Road". Although now rivalled by Huaihai Lu as a centre of commerce it is still popular with shoppers. Nanjing Donglu (Nanjing Road East), the most lively section, begins at People's Square and runs past pre-war shops, department stores, and modern boutiques all the way to the Bund, on the banks of the Huangpu River. Where Nanjing Donglu meets Nanjing Xilu is the old Shanghai Racehorse Club and clock tower, right next to Renmin Park

and the rocketing form of Tomorrow Square, housing the standout JW Marriott.

🚇 Nanjing Donglu, East Nanjing Road, People's Square
🚌 11, 14, 26

a walk around the Bund and Nanjing Road

Start your walk at the art deco Park Hotel, roughly where Nanjing Donglu meets Nanjing Xilu at the north of People's Square. Turn left out of the hotel and stroll past buildings that date from the concession days, including the renowned, old Wing On and Sincere department stores. After about half an hour you will pass the imposing, art deco Peace Hotel on your left before emerging onto the Bund, with the Huangpu River just across the way.

Of the many families of Sephardic Jews that flourished in pre-war Shanghai, the best known is the Sassoon family. The family fled from Baghdad in the 18th century to make a new life in Bombay and then proceeded to buy wharf space in Shanghai. Victor Sassoon built the Peace Hotel, a landmark on Nanjing Lu and many skyscrapers have copied its distinctive pyramidal roof design. Today's reopened and restored Peace Hotel dates from 1930,

and is an art deco icon of Shanghai. Pop in and take a look at the marvellous interior. The original furnishings were spectacular and the Horse and Hounds Bar was the most fashionable rendezvous point in the city. The glory faded throughout the rest of the 20th century and the hotel became so worn that, in early 2007, a major renovation was launched, resulting in what you see today.

Continue to the Bund and turn left, passing the Bank of China building,

the original headquarters of the former opium traders,
Jardine Matheson and the old British Consulate. At
Waibaidu Bridge, cross to the riverside embankment and
return along the Bund, past the HSBC building and the
Customs House. Walk south to the end of the Bund, just
opposite the Dong Feng Hotel, the old Shanghai Club,
and re-cross the road before walking the short distance
to Bund 5 (5 Zhongshan Dongyi Lu), home to the M on
the Bund restaurant.

Distance: 4km (2.5 miles) **Time:** 2 hours
Start point: The Park Hotel
End point and lunch: M on the Bund ($$$); 7th Floor, 20 Guangdong
Road; tel: (021) 6350 9988; www.m-onthebund.com; daily (except
Mon lunch)

Nanshi (Shanghai Old Town)

Before 1842, Shanghai was a walled town concentrated in the area sometimes called Nanshi in the Huangpu District. Unfortunately, the walls were pulled down in 1911 but modern day Renmin Lu still reflects the circular shape of the old edifice. The centre of the town was dominated by the Huxinting Teahouse, Yu Garden (➤ 120–121), and the Temple of the City God. The maze of alleyways, overhung with laundry and bounded by Remin Lu and Zhonghua Lu, are great for exploring old Shanghai. Activity centres on the Yu Garden and the Yuyuan Bazaar, around the Temple of the City God. You can also find the Confucius Temple here as well as

the delightful Chenxiangge Nunnery, while a chunk of the original city wall sits within the Dajing Pavilion. For a cup of tea, try the atmospheric Old Shanghai Teahouse (385 Fangbang Zhonglu) or the old Huxinting Teahouse, within the next to the Yu Garden.

✉ Huangpu District, southwest of the Bund

Pudong

Pudong, literally translated as "east of the Huangpu River", is Shanghai's stunning financial and commercial district. The area is lashed to Puxi by a series of vast bridges and tunnels. The most dazzling part of Pudong is Lujiazui, marked by the triumphant forms of the stratospheric **Shanghai World Financial Centre**, the dashing Jinmao Tower and the awkward but arresting Oriental Pearl TV Tower. For the best panoramic views, ascend to

the observation deck of the Shanghai World Financial Centre, the highest in the world above ground level. A few structures from the 2010 World Expo Site remain, to be used for future exhibitions.

Shanghai World Financial Centre

✉ 100 Century Avenue ☎ www.wfc-observatory.com ⏰ Daily 8am–midnight 🖐 Moderate 🚇 Lujiazui

Shanghai Bowuguan (Shanghai Museum)

The Shanghai Museum remains China's best museum with a magnificent collection of exhibits spanning the millennia.

Formally opened in 1996 on People's Square, the museum houses some 120,000 cultural relics, displayed to their best advantage by state-of-the-art lighting. The three principal permament galleries to visit are bronzes and stone sculptures, ceramics and paintings.

Other galleries are devoted to jade, Chinese coins, seals, calligraphy, traditional furniture and the art of China's minority peoples. There are also special temporary exhibition halls.

✉ 201 Renmin Dadao, Huangpu District ☎ (021) 6372 3500; www.shanghaimuseum.net ⏰ Daily 9–5 🖐 Free 🚇 People's Square 🚌 23, 49

Shanghai Dangdai Yishuguan (Shanghai Museum of Contemporary Art)

A wonderful and exciting addition to Shanghai's gallery selection, this modern museum in Renmin Park displays regular international exhibitions within a glass-walled and thoroughly modern gallery exhibiting space.

www.mocashanghai.org

✉ Renmin Park ☎ (021) 6327 9900
🕐 Daily 10–9:30 💷 Inexpensive
🚇 People's Square

Shanghai Meishuguan (Shanghai Art Museum)

It is the concession architecture and lovely exhibition space within that steal the show of the former racecourse club, a British-built edifice dating from 1933. This is one of Shanghai's many gems, and that's before you even get to the art.

www.sh-artmuseum.org.cn

✉ 325 West Nanjing Road 🕐 Daily 9–5 💷 Inexpensive 🚇 People's Square

Tianzifang

For a look at Shanghai's classic alleyway shikumen architecture while shopping at some of the town's most creative clothes outlets and sipping coffee at trendy cafes, this small tangle of lanes is the perfect alternative to Shanghai's bustling mega-malls and overbearing department stores. If you're in need of a refreshment stop, grab a coffee and read a good book at the Deke Erh Art Centre (2 Lane 210, Taikang Lu) on your left as you walk up the main alley; for artist's studios, pop into the International Artists Factory, a modern block on your right, also home to several design outfits and boutiques. Alleys branch off from the main lanes,

leading to fascinating courtyards and further alleys stuffed with small clothes boutiques, jewellery shops and restaurants.

✉ Lane 210, Taikang Lu 🕓 Daily 24 hours ✋ Free 🚇 South Shanxi Road, then taxi

Xujiahui Tianzhu Jiaotang (St Ignatius Cathedral)

Xu Guangqi, a native of Xujiahui, or Xu Family Village, and an official of the Imperial Library, was an early convert to Catholicism. Baptised Paul, he later donated family land to Jesuit missionaries from Europe for the construction of an observatory and a cathedral. Following a period of anti-Catholic persecution, the church was turned into a temple dedicated to the God of War. After the Treaty of Nanking (1842) the land was turned over to the French, and two years later a Jesuit settlement was established here. The present-day St Ignatius Cathedral dates from 1906; note the traces of Buddhist symbolism, from the melons on the nave columns and stylized bats on the windows. Do pop into the nearby **Bibliotheca Zi-Ka-Wei** reading room and try to book one of the Saturday tours of their magnificent Jesuit library.

✉ 158 Puxi Lu ☎ (021) 6253 0959 🕓 Services Mon–Sat 6:15am and 7am, Sun 6am, 7:30am, 10am and 6pm (all services in Chinese) 🚇 Xujiahui
🚌 42, 50

Bibiotheca Zi-Ka-Wei

✉ 80 Caoxi Beilu ☎ (021) 6487 4095 🕓 Library tour Sat 2–4

Yu Yuan (Yu Garden)

This exquisite garden is a fine example of a classic Ming garden, with rockeries, bridges, ponds, pavilions and corridors creating the illusion of a natural landscape or a classical Chinese painting.

The garden was created in the mid-16th century by Pan Yunduan as an act of filial affection for his father. Pan, a Shanghai native who had been in public service in Sichuan Province, must have been a wealthy figure in the city, for the garden takes up almost 5ha (12 acres). Following the death of the elder Pan in 1577, the garden fell into neglect. It was used twice as a military headquarters in the 19th century, first by Lieutenant General Gough of the British Land Force in 1842, and in the 1850s by the Small Sword Society, an offshoot of the secret Heaven and Earth Society.

✉ 132 Anren Jie, Huangpu District 🕐 Daily 8:30–5:30 👊 Moderate
🚇 Yuyuan Garden 🚌 11, 126

Xintiandi

Crafted from a 1930s French Concession shikumen (stone-gate dwelling) estate, Xintiandi is a zone of trendy bars, restaurants, shops and museums. The history of the area is explained in fascinating detail in the Shikumen Open House Museum (Sun–Thu 10:30–10:30, Fri–Sat 11–11) which reveals the interior of a typical shikumen house. Housed within a historic building is the Site of the 1st National Congress of the Chinese Communist Party (daily 9–5), where the CCP was secretly founded in 1921.

www.xintiandi.com

✉ Huangpi Nanlu, Luwan District ☎ (021) 6311 2288 🚇 South Huangpi Road 🛈 Opposite the Shikumen Open House Museum

Anhui and Henan Provinces

HUANGSHAN (YELLOW MOUNTAIN)

Rising up from the south of poverty-stricken Anhui province, Huangshan is possibly China's most attractive mountain, outside of Tibet. The peak is not one of China's sacred Buddhist or Taoist mountains, but its mists and ethereal views push it into supernatural territory. Many visitors overnight on the summit for views of the sunrise, although the climb and descent can be done in a day. Over the centuries, Huangshan's craggy peaks and pools of fog drew legions of landscape painters and photographers.

🕂 5H 🖂 70km (43 miles) north of Huangshan City (Tunxi) 🖐 Expensive 🚌 Hourly from Hangzhou, daily from Shanghai 🚆 Daily overnight train (K8418) from Shanghai to Huangshan City 🛫 Huangshan Airport (5km/3 miles west of Huangshan City)

LUOYANG

Luoyang served as China's capital and cultural centre for ten dynasties, over a period of more than 1,000 years. Today the city is an unsightly place, but Luoyang's pride and joy, the Longmen Caves, are outside town. Cave carvings date from the late fifth century but the most impressive is the

Ancestor Worshipping Cave, carved by Tang sculptors in the seventh century. The face of the huge central effigy of Buddha is said to be based on that of Tang Empress Wu Zetian, a powerful patron of Buddhism.

🕂 3F 🖂 90km (56 miles) west of Zhengzhou, Henan Province 🚌 Buses to Beijing, Kaifeng, Zhengzhou 🚆 Daily from Beijing, Shanghai, Xi'an, Zhengzhou 🛫 Luoyang Airport (12km/7.5 miles north of the city)

SHAOLIN TEMPLE

Fêted as the birthplace of China's fighting arts, Shaolin Temple dates back to AD497 and occupies a scenic spot on the western edge of Songshan, one of Taoism's five sacred mountains. Legend has it that Shaolin Boxing was developed here by Bodhidharma, a south Asian ascetic and the founder of Zen Buddhism, who began to imitate animals as a means of relaxation between meditation sessions. These exercises evolved into the "kungfu" we know today. Visit the Pilu Pavilion to see where resident monks practised their moves for centuries, and walk among the delightful Stupa Forest where hundreds of stupas commemorate eminent monks.

✚ 3F ✉ 80km (50 miles) southwest of Zhengzhou, Henan Province
☎ (0371) 6274 8971 ⏰ Daily 7–6:30 ✋ Expensive 🚌 Buses to Luoyang, Zhengzhou and Dengfeng

Jiangsu Province

NANJING

One of China's four ancient capital cities, Nanjing, on the southern bank of the Yangze River, served as capital during the Three Kingdoms period, the Song, Liang and Tang Dynasties. It became China's capital again for a brief period in the Ming Dynasty, and after 1928 when Chiang Kaishek moved his Nationalist government here. Japanese troops invaded the city in 1937, committing one of the 20th century's worst atrocities. The so-called Rape of Nanjing left an estimated 300,000 Chinese dead. In 1949, the Communists moved the capital back to Beijing.

The stunning Ming city wall still largely stands and, at 42km (26 miles) in length, is the longest in China. You can climb the wall at several points, including an excellent section to the rear of Jiming Temple. In the centre of the city is the Drum Tower, built in 1382, and the Bell Tower, which houses a bronze bell, cast in 1388. Try to see the Memorial Hall of the Nanjing

Massacre (Tue–Sun 8:30–4:30; free), where exhibits chronicle the appalling suffering meted out to the citizens of Nanjing by Japanese troops in 1937. Nearby Zijinshan (Purple and Gold Mountain) is home to many tourist sights, including Sun Yatsen's huge mausoleum, the tomb of Hongwu, first emperor of the Ming dynasty, and a working astronomical observatory.

🚉 5G ✉ Capital of Jiangsu Province, 300km (186 miles) northwest of Shanghai 🚌 Express buses to Hangzhou, Shanghai, Suzhou 🚆 Daily from Beijing, Hangzhou, Shanghai, Wuxi

SUZHOU

A city of ornamental gardens, canals and sporadic arched bridges, Suzhou is an attractive Jiangsu water town. Suzhou has a long history, but did not fully prosper until the construction of the Grand Canal during the Sui Dynasty (AD581–618). By the 12th century, Suzhou had

become a noted producer of silk. It has long been known as a centre for artists, scholars, merchants, financiers and high-ranking government officials who built fine gardens around their villas where they could enjoy a peaceful retirement. The city was damaged when it was occupied (1860–63), but it was rebuilt.

Suzhou's famous gardens are worth a visit; there is no need to see them all so focus on the Humble Administrator's Garden and the Garden of the Master of the Nets, but make sure you find time for the stunning Suzhou Museum (204 Dongbei Jie; daily 9–5; free). **http://suzhou.jiangsu.net**

🚉 5G ✉ 80km (50 miles) west of Shanghai, Jiangsu Province 🚌 Express buses to Hangzhou, Nanjing, Shanghai, Wuxi, Zhouzhuang 🚆 Regular trains throughout the day from Shanghai, also Beijing and Nanjing
🛈 North Bus Station, 29 Xihui Beilu

ZHOUZHUANG

The old town of Zhouzhuang, with quaint traditional houses standing over arched bridges and canals, lies 35km (22 miles) southwest of Suzhou. The town dates back to 1086 when a noted Buddhist, Zhou Digong, donated 13ha (32 acres) of land to the Full Fortune Temple, which later took the name of Zhouzhuang. Around 60 per cent of the houses are said to date from the Ming and Qing dynasties. For a tour of the picturesque city, explore the small alleyways or take a ride in one of the boats that follow the canals.

➕ 5G ✉ 35km southwest of Suzhou, Jiangsu Province
☎ (0512) 5721 1654; www.zhouzhuang.net ✋ Expensive
🚌 Regular buses from Suzhou and Shanghai Sightseeing Bus Centre (inside Shanghai Stadium)

Shandong Province

QINGDAO

Best places to see, ➤ 52–53.

TAISHAN

Revered for more than 2,500 years, Taishan is China's most climbed Taoist mountain. Since Taishan is the farthest east of the sacred mountains, the Chinese believed that the sun began its daily trip westward from here, and 72 emperors have performed rituals at Taishan. The climb to the top includes 7,000 stone steps leading to the 1,560m (5,118ft) summit, or there is a cable car. Over the centuries, more than 250 Taoist and Buddhist temples and monuments were built here.

➕ 4E ✉ Tai'an City, 64km (40 miles) north of Qufu, Shandong Province ✋ Expensive 🚌 Regular services from Jinan and Qufu
🚉 Tai'an Railway Station 🚐 Minibuses from Qufu

QUFU

The birthplace of Confucius (551–479BC), Qufu was the capital of the state of Lu at the time of the Master's birth. After the death of Confucius, Emperor Han Wudi built a temple to honour the great Master. Today, about 100,000 of the city's more than 500,000 residents claim the Kong family name (Confucius' surname was Kong). The main sight is the Confucius Temple, the largest of its kind in China, which centres on the huge Dacheng Hall, notable for its magnificently carved columns. The Apricot Altar is the site where Confucius taught his students. The adjacent Kong Family Mansion is where family members lived until 1937. The mansion was first built in 1068, but the present structures were built in the Ming and Qing dynasties.

The Confucius Cemetery, north of Qufu, is the site of some 100,000 Kong tombs, with Confucius buried in the centre of the cemetery. His son,

Kong Li, is buried to the east, and his grandson to the south.

✚ 4F ✉ Shandong Province 🚌 Buses to Yanzhou 16km (10 miles) to the west, Tai'an, Jinan and Qingdao

🚆 Yanzhou

❓ The Confucius Cultural Festival, 26 Sep–10 Oct

Zhejiang Province

HANGZHOU

Hangzhou, an old imperial capital, is renowned for its serene beauty. Marco Polo, who visited here in the 13th century, called it the most beautiful and prosperous city in the world. Many artists flocked here, transforming it into a cultural centre. Two of China's most famous poets, Tang poet Bai Juyi and Song poet Su Dongpo, served as mayors. Hangzhou continued to prosper during the Ming and Qing eras due to the thriving silk industry and its location in a fertile rice-growing region. The city was attacked

by pirates in the 16th century, and was damaged during the Taiping Rebellion in the 19th century.

The main tourist attraction is West Lake, encircled by misty green hills where Longjing tea and mulberry trees are cultivated. Originally a humble lagoon, West Lake was dredged in the eighth century and later diked. It is one of the few attractions in China that you won't need to pay for the pleasure of viewing. The Su Causeway, named after Su Dongpo, is a good place to enjoy the lake's scenery.

Explore the hills north of West Lake for the Baochu Pagoda and excellent views over the water. West of the lake is Hangzhou's premier Buddhist temple, the excellent Lingyin Temple, which dates from the fourth century. Nearby is The Peak that Flew from Afar, containing Buddhist rock carvings. The Temple of Yue Fei on the lake's north shore is dedicated to a Song Dynasty general.

⊞ 5H ✉ Capital of Zhejiang Province, 175km (109 miles) southwest of Shanghai 🚌 Express buses to Nanjing, Shanghai 🚆 Daily from Shanghai (throughout the day), Beijing, Guangzhou ✈ Hangzhou Airport (15km/9 miles) from city centre

ℹ Hangzhou Railway Station; tel: (0571) 8782 5755

PUTUOSHAN

Putuoshan, one of China's four sacred Buddhist mountains, is a hilly island about 6km (4 miles) long and 5km (3 miles) wide, with its highest point the 286m-tall (938ft) Buddha's Peak. Famed for its views and balmy weather, the island is strongly associated with Guanyin, the Buddhist bodhisattva of mercy, worshipped in island's three main temples: Puji Temple in the south and Fayu Temple and Huiji Temple farther north. Huiji Temple is quite small, but interesting for the climb up the slopes of Buddha's Peak to the temple from Fayu Temple below. A huge golden statue of the Southsea Guanyin rises up from the southeast tip of the island.

⊞ 6H ✉ Zhejiang Province, East China Sea ✋ Expensive 🚢 Regular boats from Ningbo, fast boats and overnight boat from Shanghai ✈ Zhujiajian Island

HOTELS

HANGZHOU
Shangri-La Hotel ($$$)
Beautifully located amid lush gardens and overlooking Hangzhou's famed West Lake. With a fitness centre, snooker and billiards hall, swimming pool and sauna this is the best-equipped hotel in town.
✉ 78 Beishan Lu ☎ (0571) 8797 7951; www.shangri-la.com

HUANGSHAN
Beihai Binguan ($$)
The best hotel for those wanting to catch the sunrise or sunset from the top of the mountain. It's a 20-minute walk away from the White Goose Peak cable car. Facilities are adequate.
✉ Beihai Scenic Area, eastern steps of the mountain ☎ (0559) 558 2555; www.beihaihotel.com

LUOYANG
Peony Hotel ($$)
Located at the heart of Luoyang this hotel has attractive, spacious rooms with satellite television and air-conditioning. Other facilities include a sauna and an excellent restaurant, the Mudan Ting.
✉ 15 Zhongzhou Xilu ☎ (0379) 6468 0000

NANJING
Jinling Fandian ($$–$$$)
Probably the best local hotel in town, located in the very heart of bustling Nanjing. Swimming pool, sauna and steam room, shopping arcade and a number of excellent restaurants.
✉ 2 Hanzhong Lu, Xinjiekou Square ☎ (025) 8471 1888; www.jinlinghotel.com

QINGDAO
Shangri-La Hotel ($$$)
In the east of the town, this typically plush and elegant member of the elite Shangri-La chain has an indoor pool, fitness centre, tennis courts and the famed Shang Palace Cantonese restaurant.
✉ 9 Xianggang Zhonglu ☎ (0532) 8388 3838; www.shangri-la.com

QUFU
Queli Hotel ($–$$)
Just a stone's throw from the famous Confucian Temple. The staff greet visitors with one of Confucius's famous quotes, "It is wonderful to have friends from afar!" All rooms have satellite television and minibar.
✉ 1 Queli Jie ☎ (0537) 486 6818; www.quelihotel.com

PUTUOSHAN
Putuoshan Hotel ($$)
The best hotel on the island has a scenic location in between the pier and the Puji Temple. The hotel is simple, but elegant, in style.
✉ 93 Meicen Lu ☎ (0580) 609 2828; www.putuoshanhotel.com

SHANGHAI
Captain Hostel ($)
Perhaps not the very best hostel in town, but possibly the most popular and also the best positioned, just a few steps from the Bund, plus a winning terrace bar with jaw-dropping views.
✉ 37 Fuzhou Lu ☎ (021) 6323 5053; www.captainhostel.com.cn

Mingtown Hiker Youth Hostel ($)
With some excellent value and well-presented double rooms, and a top position a short walk from the Bund, this is a popular hostel.
✉ 450 Jiangxi Zhonglu ☎ (021) 6329 7889

Old House Inn ($$)
This charming old property down an alley on the edge of the French Concession has been thoughtfully converted, with period charms and only a dozen rooms.
✉ 16 Lane 351, off Huashan Lu ☎ (021) 6248 6118; www.oldhouse.cn

Park Hyatt ($$$)
See page 63.

Peace Hotel ($$$)
See page 63.

The Portman Ritz-Carlton ($$$)

Winner of numerous "Best Hotel" awards this giant hotel caters for all tastes with health club, shopping mall and 24-hour business centre. Also houses the renowned Summer Pavilion Restaurant.

✉ Shanghai Centre, 1376 Nanjingxi Lu ☎ (021) 6279 8888; www.ritzcarlton.com

Pudi Boutique Hotel ($$)

See page 63.

SUZHOU
Bamboo Grove Hotel ($–$$)

Despite having its own garden, the Bamboo Grove Hotel is well set for many of Suzhou's more famous gardens. Comfortable and friendly, it has a gym, tennis courts, sauna and swimming pool.

✉ 168 Zuhui Lu ☎ (0512) 6520 5601; www.bg-hotel.com

RESTAURANTS

HANGZHOU
Louwailou ($$)

Located with excellent views of West Lake. Specialties include West Lake *xihu cuyu* (vinegar fish), *dongpo rou* (pork slices cooked with Shaoxing wine), longjing shrimp and beggar's chicken.

✉ 30 Gushan Lu ☎ (0571) 8796 9023; www.louwailou.com.cn
🕙 Daily lunch and dinner

Zhiweiguan Restaurant ($)

This simple restaurant offers popular local snacks from noodles to boiled and steamed dumplings. Try cat's ears – small triangles of dough snipped off into a boiling pot, and served in a broth.

✉ 83 Renhe Lu ☎ (0571) 870 8638 🕙 Daily breakfast, lunch and dinner

NANJING
Qinhuai Renjia ($)

Plain cafeteria style eatery on Dashiba Jie, one of the atmospheric "old streets" close to the Confucius Temple (Fuzi Miao) area.

✉ 128 Dashiba Jie, Fuzi Miao ☎ (025) 5221 1888 🕙 Daily lunch and dinner

PUTUOSHAN
Zhongshan Fandian ($)
In keeping with the Buddhist spirit of Putuoshan, this restaurant serves up excellent vegetarian food, as well as some excellent seafood dishes.

✉ 19 Xiangyun Lu, beside the Fayu Temple, Putuoshan ☎ (0580) 669 0899
🕐 Daily lunch and dinner

QINGDAO
Tianfu Laoma ($$)
Decorated in a traditional style, this restaurant is a favourite with locals and serves dishes that originated from several of the Chinese schools of cooking, from Sichuan-style hot pot to eastern seafood specialities.

✉ 54 Yunxiao Lu, Shinan District ☎ (0532) 8576 4906 🕐 Daily lunch and dinner

SHANGHAI
Bi Feng Tang ($)
With branches in prize locations around Shanghai, this restaurant serves up great value Cantonese Dim Sum dishes in a bright, festive environment. Menus at Bi Feng Tang are in English.

✉ 1333 Nanjing Xilu, close to Tongren Lu ☎ (021) 6279 0738
🕐 Daily breakfast, lunch and dinner

Dongbei Ren ($)
Donbei Ren serves up fun peasant-style food over two crowded storeys. Order the Squirrel Fish and the smart waiting staff will sing and clap as food is bought to your table.

✉ 46 Panyu Lu [by Yanan Xilu] ☎ (021) 5230 2230; www.dongbeiren.com
🕐 Daily lunch and dinner

Lynn ($$)
See page 59

M on the Bund ($$$)
See page 59.

Old Shanghai Teahouse ($)

Just south of the Yu Garden in the old town, this great upstairs teahouse is littered with period effects, antiques and bric-a-brac, conjuring up a distinctive mood.

✉ 385 Fangbang Zhonglu, old town 🕐 Daily 9–9

Sasha's ($$)

Ensconced within a beautiful 1920s French Concession villa, Sasha's offers European food and wine in an elegant setting.

✉ 11 Dongping Lu (near Hengshan Lu) ☎ (021) 6474 6628; www.sashas-shanghai.com 🕐 Daily lunch and dinner

Vegetarian Lifestyle ($–$$)

You'll find meat-free, organic and MSG-devoid Chinese food here – flavoursome and imaginative. The much-loved restaurant has many regularly returning customers and two further branches.

✉ 258 Fengxian Lu ☎ (021) 6215 7566 🕐 Daily 10–9

Yang's Kitchen ($$)

Great Shanghai home-style cooking is served here. The restaurant is in a refined setting.

✉ No 3, Alley 9, Hengshan Lu (near the intersection of Dongping Lu) ☎ (021) 6445 8418 🕐 Daily lunch and dinner

SUZHOU
Songhelou ($)

The long-established Songhelou is known for its eastern Chinese seafood cooking. Other branches around the city.

✉ 72 Taijian Lu, off Guanqian Jie ☎ (0512) 6727 7006 🕐 Daily lunch and dinner

SHOPPING

SHANGHAI
Chinese Printed Blue Nankeen Exhibition Hall

Hidden away at the end of a lane, this hall and shop has an assortment of printed traditional blue and white cloth designs.

✉ No. 24, Lane 637, Changle Lu ☎ (021) 5403 7947 🕐 Daily 9–5

Fuyou Market

Shanghai's most famous antiques market. The best bargains can be had early mornings at weekends. Bargaining is a must.

✉ Fangbang Zhonglu (near Henan Nanlu), Huangpu District 🕐 Daily 9–5 approx. Open from 5am Sat–Sun

Hongqiao International Pearl City

Large shopping centre stuffed with smaller vendors who allow you to commission your own jewellery or buy ready-made items.

✉ 3721 Hongmei Lu (by Yan'an Xilu), Minhang District ☎ (021) 6465 0000; www.hqpearl.com

Madame Mao's Dowry

Trendy cache of collectibles from the Cultural Revolution and antiques from dynastic China.

✉ 207 Fumin Lu ☎ (021) 5403 3551 🕐 Daily 1–7

Shanghai South Bund Fabric Market

Bespoke clothing can be stitched together amazingly quickly here.

✉ 399 Lujiabang Lu, Huangpu district ☎ (021) 6377 2236 🕐 Daily 8:30–6

Suzhou Cobblers

Exquisite hand-embroidered Chinese silk slippers and handbags in a range of colours and designs.

✉ Room 101, 17 Fuzhou Lu ☎ (021) 6329 9656; www.suzhou-cobblers.com

Torana House

This indie shop specializes in handmade wool rugs from Tibet and places along the former Silk Road.

✉ 164 Anfu Lu ☎ (021) 5404 4886; www.toranahouse.com 🕐 Daily 10:30–7

ART GALLERIES
Shanghai Museum Shop

A large collection of tasteful art reproductions, paintings, stationery, books and more. Worth visiting if you're in the museum.

✉ Shanghai Museum, 201 Renmin Lu, Shanghai ☎ (021) 6372 3500; www.shanghaimuseum.net

BOOKS
Shanghai Foreign Languages Bookstore
All kinds of foreign language books, primarily in English, but some in Spanish, French and other languages, as well as CDs and videos, can be found here.

✉ 390 Fuzhou Lu, Shanghai ☎ (021) 6322 3200

Garden Books
Sells a wide range of imported titles, as well as international ones. Also has an ice-parlour on the ground floor.

✉ 325 Changle Lu, Shanghai ☎ (021) 5404 8728

DEPARTMENT STORES
Plaza 66
More than 100 international designer brands have a home in this trendy mall, close to the Shanghai Centre. It's a good place for an entire day's shopping.

✉ 1266 Nanjing Xilu (near Jiangning Lu) ☎ (021) 6279 0910
🕓 Daily 10–10

Isetan
This Japanese-run department store is on one of Shanghai's main shopping drags. Among its ranges are international, Japanese and local products.

✉ 537 Huaihai Zhonglu, Shanghai ☎ (021) 5306 1111 🕓 Mon–Fri 10–9, Sat–Sun 10–9:30

Shanghai No 1 Department Store
This old pre-liberation stalwart department store has an enormous range of products.

✉ 830 Nanjing Donglu, Shanghai ☎ (021) 6322 3344 🕓 Daily 9:30am–10pm

SHOPPING STREETS
Nanjing Donglu, Shanghai
Packed with small shops, boutiques and department stores, this bustling commercial centre is at the heart of the modern city of Shanghai.

ENTERTAINMENT

ARTS

Garden of the Master of the Nets

Nightly performances including traditional local opera, dance and theatre. The audience moves around the gardens.

✉ 11 Kuojiatou Xiang (front gate) or Shiquan Jie (back gate), Suzhou
☎ (0512) 6520 3514 🕐 Daily 7:30–9:30pm

Shanghai Concert Hall

This is the home of the Shanghai Symphony Orchestra. Check local listings magazines for performances.

✉ 523 Yan'an Donglu, Shanghai ☎ (021) 6386 2836; www.culture.sh.cn

Shanghai Dramatic Arts Centre

A small theatre with consistently good productions, and some performances in English. Check the website for current events.

✉ 288 Anfu Lu, Shanghai ☎ (021) 6473 4567; www.china-drama.com

Shanghai Grand Theatre

A huge, modern international opera house with a spectacular curved roof. The building contains three separate theatres.

✉ 300 Renmin Dadao, Shanghai ☎ (021) 6386 8686; www.shgtheatre.com

Shanghai Centre Theatre

Home to the Shanghai Acrobatics Troupe who put on a daily hour-and-a-half show. Occasionally a venue for music concerts.

✉ 1376 Nanjing Xilu ☎ (021) 6279 8948 🕐 Shows begin at 7:30pm

Studio City

Large, modern movie hall with six screens showing all the latest blockbusters. Soundtracks in Chinese and English.

✉ 10th Floor Westgate Mall, 1038 Nanjingxi Lu, Shanghai ☎ (021) 6218 2173

Yifu Theatre

The great stars of traditional Beijing Opera perform here.

✉ 701 Fuzhou Lu, Shanghai ☎ (021) 6322 5294; www.tianchan.com
🕐 Performances Fri and Sat eve, Sun matinee

NIGHTLIFE
Barbarossa
Rising up next to the pond within Renmin Park, this Moroccan-themed bar is ideal for unwinding to great tunes and puffing on hookah pipes.

✉ Renmin Park, 231 Nanjing Xilu ☎ (021) 6318 0220 ⊕ Daily 11am–2am

New Heights ($)
Put yourself up there with the best: it's a tall order not to be won over by this great bar-cum-restaurant's top-drawer night-time Shanghai views.

✉ 7th floor, Three on the Bund, 3 Zhongshan Dong Yilu, Shanghai ☎ (021) 6321 0909 ⊕ Daily noon–10:30

O'Malley's Irish Pub
This intimate bar, located in an old Shanghai mansion, has an elegant hardwood interior and authentic Irish antiques. An ideal place for enjoying a drink outdoors in the warm weather.

✉ 42 Taojiang Lu, Shanghai ☎ (021) 6474 4533; www.omalleys-shanghai.com ⊕ Daily 24 hours

SPORT

Disc Kart Indoor Karting
This is the largest indoor go-kart racing track, covering 4,500sq m (5,382sq yds), in Asia.

✉ 809 Zaoyang Lu, near Jinshajing Lu line 3 metro station, Shanghai ☎ (021) 6222 2880; www.kartingchina.com ⊕ Daily 2pm–2am

IB Racing Kart Club
Outdoor leisure karts and top-end racing go-karts are offered here.

✉ 880 Zhongshan Beiyilu, inside Quyang Park, Hongkou District, Shanghai ☎ (021) 6531 6800; www.quyangkart.com ⊕ Daily 10–10

Masterhand Rock Climbing Club
Indoor and outdoor rock climbing, mountaineering and camping.

✉ No 21, Upper Stand, Hongkou Football Stadium, 444 Dongjiangwan Lu, Shanghai ☎ (021) 5696 6657 ⊕ Daily 10–10

Hong Kong and Southern China

Hong Kong serves up an exotic entrée to the China experience, blending Western comforts with Chinese verve. However, there is much more to the southern part of China than this waterfront metropolis.

Hong Kong

Known primarily as a city destination, Hong Kong's landscapes are often overlooked. The spectacular skyline of Hong Kong Island contrasts sharply with the rugged wilderness of Lantau Island.

The province that wraps around Hong Kong is Guangdong – crucible of Cantonese culture and home to famously fine food.

Nearby Hainan Island is a tropical treat, blessed with blue skies, great sand beaches and a bevy of beautiful hotels.

Moving deeper into the south, the landscape and inhabitants become more diverse. The provinces of Guangxi and Guizhou boast soaring rice terraces, sugarloaf karst mountains and diverse minority communities, each with their own traditions, costumes, language and culture. Fujian Province has a large Hakka population, distinguished for its unusual architecture. Hunan, meanwhile, sets itself apart with food. Mao Zedong's home province is known for its affection for chilli peppers.

HONG KONG

Best places to see, ➤ 44–45.

Hong Kong Island

What Queen Victoria once called a useless lump of rock has long been the high rise-studded symbol of Asian affluence. The island represents only a fraction of Hong Kong's overall bulk but a lot of money, power and people are packed into its limited confines. The district of Central is where most deals are done. The 88-storey Two IFC office tower dominates the skyline but there are smaller gems worth seeking out, like the Legislative Council Building. Lan Kwai Fong and surrounding streets have the best bars in town, while catching the **Peak Tram** up to Victoria Peak is an essential experience. Also find time to ride the Mid-Levels Escalator up to the trendy Soho district. Sheung Wan is a

more traditionally Chinese district, with musty old shops selling herbal remedies and dried seafood. The southern half of the island is green and hilly with quaint seaside towns. Stanley has a market, while Aberdeen is home to Ocean Park amusements (➤ 66).

➕ 4L

Peak Tram

✉ 33 Garden Road, Central (behind St John's Building) ☎ (852) 2522 0922; www.thepeak.com.hk 🕐 Daily 7–midnight 💰 Inexpensive 🚇 Central
🚌 15, 15B, 15C, 515

Kowloon

Kowloon is the land to the north of Victoria Harbour. The district at the southern tip is known as Tsim Sha Tsiu, or TST for short, and is home to a cluster of cultural buildings and museums (➤ 143) and the Peninsula Hong Kong hotel. Inland is the excellent **Hong Kong Museum of History.** The maze of streets farther north is a different proposition. The slick sophistication of Hong Kong Island is replaced by a riot of commercialism set against a backdrop of crumbling tenement blocks and crackling neon signs. Nathan Road is the main vein that runs from the waterfront to Boundary Road. Temple Street Night Market (6pm–midnight) is Hong Kong's most famous night market. Farther north is the **Chi Lin Nunnery**.

➕ 4L

Chi Lin Nunnery

✉ 5 Chi Lin Drive, Diamond Hill ☎ (852) 2354 1888; www.chilin.org
🕐 Convent: Daily 9–4, Lotus Pond Garden: Daily 7–9 💰 Free 🚇 Diamond Hill

Hong Kong Museum of History

✉ 100 Chatham Road South ☎ (852) 2724 9042 🕐 Mon, Wed–Sat 10–6, Sun 10–7. Closed Tue 💰 Inexpensive 🚇 Tsim Sha Tsui

Lantau Island

With its mountainous interior and rocky coastline, Lantau has long been has long been popular for its beaches and outdoor excursion possibilities. If you are feeling energetic, embark on the breezy Lantau Trail across the island. Of modern construction, the 26m (85ft) tall **Tian Tan Buddha** at the vast Po Lin Monastery is the world's largest seated bronze Buddha, offering fantastic views. **Hong Kong Disneyland** is built on reclaimed land towards Lantau's eastern tip. The **Ngong Ping 360** cable car conveys you on a 5.7km (3.5 miles) ride from Tung Chung to Ngong Ping village at thrillingly steep angles.

Ngong Ping Village is billed as a "traditional Chinese village" but features a host of Western chain stores. Elsewhere on Lantau, Mui Wo and Tai O are pleasant fishing villages that offer a different take on Hong Kong life.

➕ 3L

Tian Tan Buddha

✉ Ngong Ping Village ☎ (852) 2985 5248 🕐 Daily 10–6 ✋ Free 🚌 2 from Mui Wo, 21 from Tai O, 23 from Tung Chung

Hong Kong Disneyland

✉ Lantau Island ☎ (852) 1833 0830; http://park.hongkongdisneyland.com 🕐 See website as times vary ✋ Adult HK$350, child HK$250

Ngong Ping Skyrail

✉ Tung Chung ☎ (852) 2109 9898; www.np360.com.hk 🕐 Mon–Fri 10–6, Sat–Sun 9–6:30 ✋ Moderate 🚌 Tung Chung

Victoria Harbour

This famous passage between Hong Kong Island and Kowloon is now only around half of its original 2km (1.25 miles) width due to extensive land reclamation. Nevertheless, the Star Ferry ride across the harbour remains one of the world's great boat trips. It may be only nine minutes in duration but the views are breathtaking. North of Central Plaza is the Hong Kong Convention & Exhibition Centre, its impressive wing poking out into the harbour waters. The Kowloon side of the harbour, meanwhile, is home to another world-class performance venue, the Hong Kong Cultural Centre. The two adjacent buildings, the **Hong Kong Museum of Art** and the **Hong Kong Space Museum** (complete with planetarium) combine to make this Hong Kong's most cultured locale.

✚ 4L

Hong Kong Museum of Art, Hong Kong Space Museum
✉ 10 Salisbury Road, TST ☎ (852) 2721 0116 🕐 Sun–Wed, Fri 10–6, Sat 10–8 ✋ Inexpensive (free on Wednesdays) 🚇 Tsim Sha Tsui

Guangdong Province

GUANGZHOU (CANTON)

With its long coastline, Guangdong Province has served as the door for foreigners seeking to penetrate China for more than 1,000 years. Guangzhou, the sprawling provincial capital, today retains traces of its multicultural past in its fascinating mix of colonial and traditional Chinese architecture.

Indian and Roman traders sailed up the Pearl River to buy silk, porcelain, tea and spices in the second century. They were followed during the Tang Dynasty by Arab, Jewish, Christian and Zoroastrian merchants and, in the 15th century, by European traders and missionaries. Canton was also the jumping-off point for many Chinese who sailed to Southeast Asia and other destinations in the 19th century. The Qing court attempted to put an end to Britain's lucrative opium trade in 1839, when Commissioner Lin Zexu destroyed opium captured from Western traders. The British quickly routed China in the Opium War, which resulted in the signing of the Treaty of Nanking, and the opening of Canton and four other cities as treaty ports for foreign trade.

The city of Canton has also played a key role in the modern revolutionary history of China. The Taiping rebellion, which almost succeeded in toppling the Qing, was launched by Hong Xiuquan who came under Christian influences in Canton. Nationalist hero Sun Yatsen, who was born in nearby Zhongshan, used Canton as a base for a number of uprisings. It also has an important place in modern China. Since Deng Xiaoping's economic reforms were launched in 1979, Guangzhou has been pivotal in driving China's economy upwards.

 3L

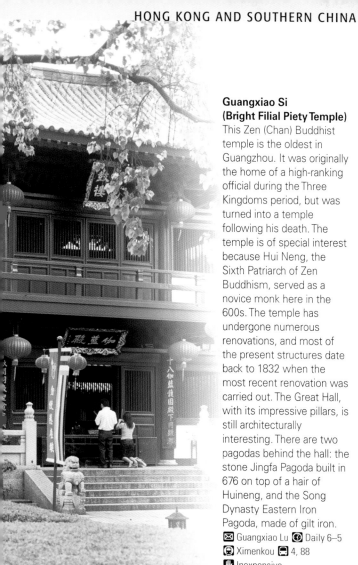

Guangxiao Si (Bright Filial Piety Temple)

This Zen (Chan) Buddhist temple is the oldest in Guangzhou. It was originally the home of a high-ranking official during the Three Kingdoms period, but was turned into a temple following his death. The temple is of special interest because Hui Neng, the Sixth Patriarch of Zen Buddhism, served as a novice monk here in the 600s. The temple has undergone numerous renovations, and most of the present structures date back to 1832 when the most recent renovation was carried out. The Great Hall, with its impressive pillars, is still architecturally interesting. There are two pagodas behind the hall: the stone Jingfa Pagoda built in 676 on top of a hair of Huineng, and the Song Dynasty Eastern Iron Pagoda, made of gilt iron.

✉ Guangxiao Lu 🕐 Daily 6–5
🚇 Ximenkou 🚌 4, 88
✋ Inexpensive

Liurongsi (Six Banyan Trees Temple)

The name of this temple comes from a poem written by Song poet Su Dongpo, who visited it in 1100, and was moved by the beauty of the trees in the courtyard, long since disappeared. Su wrote a two-character inscription – six banyans – which is now engraved on a tablet at the entrance. The nine-storey Flower Pagoda was built in the 11th century.

✉ Liurong Lu ⏰ Daily 8–5 🚌 56
✋ Inexpensive

Shamian Dao (Shamian Island)

Guangzhou's top sight, this tiny island in the southwest was established as a foreign concession in the 19th century.
Cross the footbridge and everything changes: traffic disappears, birdsong strikes up and Guangzhou's hectic mood evaporates. The central boulevard, Shamian Dajie, runs nearly the length of the

island and makes for a pleasant stroll among the various examples of French and British architecture. Great views across the Pearl River lure t'ai chi practitioners at dawn.

✉ South of Liu'ersan Lu
🚇 Huangsha

MACAU

The Portuguese leased Macau from China in 1557, and administered it until 1999, when it was returned to China. Composed of a tiny sliver of mainland peninsula and two small islands, Macau was once a booming trade port, but was later eclipsed by nearby Hong Kong. Macau today is a mixture of quaint Portuguese architecture, with interesting old forts, churches and colonial

mansions. It's also become something of an Eastern Las Vagas, thanks to the recent liberalization of the casino industry.

Macau is famous for excellent Portuguese cuisine and laid-back ambience. The stunning facade of St Paul's Cathedral is regarded as the symbol of Macau. Nearby Monte Fort is home to the excellent **Museum of Macau.** The Macanese can now boast their own theme park in the form of **Fisherman's Wharf.** This waterside project features rollercoasters and a flame-erupting volcano 40m (131ft) tall. The nearby Macau Tower has a variety of heart-stopping sky walks and bungee-assisted rides.

➕ 3L 🖂 60km (37 miles) west of Hong Kong 🚢 Regular ferries and hydrofoils from Hong Kong ❓ Macau Arts Festival, Mar

Museum of Macau

🖂 Inside Monte Fort ☎ (853) 2835 7911; www.macaumuseum.gov.mo
🕐 Tue–Sun 10–6 ✋ Inexpensive

Fisherman's Wharf

🖂 Avenida Doutor Sun Yat Sen ☎ (853) 299 3300;
www.fishermanswharf.com.mo 🕐 Open access

Fujian Province

GULANGYU ISLAND, XIAMEN

Possibly mainland China's most charming island, hilly Gulangyu is a
five-minute hop from Xiamen and a veritable museum of European
concession-era villas, churches and old embassy buildings, criss-
crossed by lazy backstreets. With no cars, it's a joy just to saunter
around the island, or check into a Gulangyu hotel and take it easy
for a few days.

Take in the former British Consulate building not far from the pier and the pure-white Roman Catholic church, not far away. Sunlight Rock offers terrific views of the island and the sea. The old eight-sided Bagua Building now contains the organ museum (daily 8:30–5). The Zheng Chenggong Museum is devoted to relics relating to the Ming loyalist and rebel who was based here. For lunch and dinner, restaurants cluster in the streets near the pier.

 5K ✉ 5-min ferry ride from Xiamen City 🚌 Electric buggies on island 🚉 Xiamen Station ⛴ Ferry from the pier opposite Lujiang Harbourview Hotel. Ferry tours along the coast ✈ Xiamen Airport

WUYI SHAN (WUYI MOUNTAIN)

A two-hour trip on a bamboo raft floating downstream from Star Village is the best way to tour picturesque Wuyi Mountain, one of China's 40 UNESCO World Heritage Sites. The journey takes you along the wonderful Nine Bends River past soaring peaks, unique rock formations, lush bamboo groves and some stunning waterfalls.

The river is also known for the boat-shaped coffins sitting in depressions on the cliffs, said to belong to the Yue, a tribe of people who lived here some 3,500 years ago. Look out for them as you sail by. Zhu Xi, the Song dynasty Confucian scholar, lived on Wuyi Mountain for many years and founded the Ziyang Academy below Yinping Peak.

The wider Wuyi Reserve has a wide variety of flora and fauna and is a great place for hiking and birdwatching.

✚ 5J ✉ Northwest Fujian Province 🕐 Daily 6:30–6:30 ✋ Expensive 🚉 Daily from Quanzhou and Xiamen ✈ Airport south of Wuyishan City

YONGDING

The countryside in Yongding, Fujian Province, is dotted with circular, oval and square fortress-type villages built over 300 years by the Hakka, a Han ethnic minority, to protect themselves from attack. Many Hakka families still live in these largely circular dwellings, known locally as *tulou* (earth houses). They are simple but solid buildings made of packed earth. The largest is capable of housing more than 1,000 people. Each building comes with a hall, kitchen, storehouse, bedrooms and a well for water.

The Hakka have their own dialect and customs. Unlike other Han women, Hakka women never followed the custom of binding their feet.

The county was named Yongding, "forever settled", at the end of Ming Dynasty, when Hakka refugees fled here to escape from war. About 20,000 *tulou* remain in the countryside, providing a startling sight when spotted from mountain roads above. Some of the finest examples of *tulou* architecture are at **Chengqilou,** Qiaofulou, Zhengfulou, and Huaijilou. The best way to view the buildings is to hire a car and driver; you can spend the night in a building for a frugal but unique experience.

🕂 4K ✉ Southwest Fujian Province 🚌 Regular buses from Guangzhou, Xiamen. Minibuses from Yongding to Chengqilou

Chengqilou

✉ A 30-min taxi ride north of Yongding 🕒 Daily 24 hours 💰 Inexpensive

Guangxi Province

GUILIN

The beautiful limestone karst scenery of Guilin has been celebrated throughout history. There are notable peaks within the city, including the 152m (500ft) tall Solitary Beauty Peak (Duxiu Feng) and Folded Brocade Hill (Diecai Shan) in the northeast of the city, as well as Seven Star Park (Qixing Gongyuan). However, the focal point of any visit must be the Li River boat ride between Yangshuo and Guilin where hundreds of sugarloaf-shaped mountains rear up from the riverbank.

Many of Guilin's karst peaks contain fabulous caves with magnificent stalagmites and stalactites. It's easy to reach them by bicycle. It is also possible to take a trip with a fisherman using cormorants to catch fish. The trained birds – which have a leash around their necks to keep them from swallowing their catch – dive for fish and then deposit their catch on the bamboo raft. The main ethnic group here is the Zhuang, the largest of China's 55 minority groups.

🕇 2K 🖂 590km (367 miles) northwest of Guangzhou, Guangxi Province 🚌 Buses from Yangshuo, Nanning 🚊 Guilin Train Station ✈ Guilin International Airport

Li River Cruise

🖂 All cruises begin at the Zhujiang (Bamboo River) Pier, 20km (12.5 miles) southeast of Guilin ☎ (0773) 282 5502 🕐 Daily 8:40am, 9:20am, 10:10am
✋ Expensive (includes lunch and return by bus)

YANGSHUO

Best places to see, ➤ 54–55.

Guizhou Province

ANSHUN

This pleasant city, set amid limestone karst hills, is a major jumping off point for two of Guizhou's most spectacular sights. Around 120km (75 miles) north of Anshun is the **Zhijin Cave.** At 10km (6 miles) in length, and with cathedral-like galleries that reach a height of 150m (492ft) in parts, Zhijin is one of the largest caves in the world. Southwest of Anshun are the **Huangguoshu Falls.** With a width of 81m (88yds) and a height of 74m (80yds), the main waterfall is one of most spectacular in China. Within the surrounding hills is a matrix of caves and underground streams. The best time to visit Anshun is between May and October.

✚ 1K

🚌 Buses to Guiyang 🚆 Services to Kunming, nearby Guiyang and Chongqing

Zhijin Cave

✉ 15km (9 miles) north of Zhijin Town ☎ (0857) 781 2063 🕐 8:30–5:30

🚌 Buses to Zhijin from Anshun. Minibuses to Zhijin Cave

Huangguoshu Falls

✉ 45km (28 miles) southwest of Anshun ☎ (0853) 359 2766 🕐 6:30am–7pm

🚌 Regular buses from Anshun 💰 Expensive

QINGYAN

The capital of Guizhou province is not terribly inspiring, but this small Ming dynasty town around 30km (18.5 miles) to the south of Guiyang has considerable historic appeal. With a town wall, town gates, watchtowers, decorative arches, traditional architecture and alleyways, Qingyan has managed to maintain a considerable amount of its historic charm.

✚ 1K ✉ Guizhou Province 🚌 Local bus from Guiyang to Qingyan via Huaxi

ZHAOXING

Zhaoxing is the largest of the many Dong villages that pepper the rice terraced hills of Guizhou's southeastern fringe. The village is divided into five sections, each belonging to a different Dong clan and each with its own wooden drum tower and Wind and Rain Bridge. These attractive bridges function as lively outdoor social clubs, capable of standing up to anything Guizhou's temperamental weather can throw at them – hence their name. Evening cultural performances feature choral singing and lusheng bamboo pipe music that seems as much about entertaining the locals as about pleasing tourists.

✚ 2K ✉ Guizhou Province 🚌 Express buses connect nearby Kaili with Guiyang; buses to Zhaoxing from Kaili via Congjiang, and Sanjiang
🚉 Nearest station in Kaili ✈ Nearest airports in Guiyang and Guilin

Hainan Province

SANYA

Located on the southern tip of Hainan, Sanya has become a playground for China's fast-emerging jet set. With white sand beaches, whispering palm trees and a slew of top hotels, Hainan is avidly marketed as the "Hawaii of the Orient". The glamour of Hainan's natural surroundings is topped up in November when Sanya frequently plays host to the annual Miss World competition.

Hainan may not have Hawaii's fearsome breakers, but the tranquil ocean is perfect for windsurfing, jet-skiing, snorkelling and scuba-diving. Hainan is home to three of China's 55 minority groups and examples of their distinctive cultures can be found in the highland villages. A word of caution, however: the commercialization of minority culture – a problem throughout China – is particularly acute around Sanya. For a more authentic experience, head inland.

♦ 5M (inset) ✉ Sanya City, Hainan Island 🚌 Regular services to Haikou 🚆 A high-speed rail line opened in 2010, connecting Haikou with Sanya (1 hour 40 min) ✈ Sanya International Airport

Hunan Province

WULINGYUAN

Wulingyuan is nature's reflection of China's newfangled high-rise cities. Around 3,000 quartzite spires shoot up from a deep valley vault, each a gravity defying compression of slate. This stunning national park in northwest Hunan Province is one of China's most remarkable geological oddities. The expensive 248RMB ticket buys two days' entry to Wulingyuan, and free use of the bus network inside the park. Visit each of the park's three areas: Zhangjiajie Forest Park, Tianzi Mountain and the Suoxi Valley are connected by trails. Stone staircases allow fitter visitors to climb to the peaks. There are two cable cars but the highlight has to be the Bailong Lift (Bailong Dianti). It is attached to a sheer rock face and whisks guests up 326m (1,070ft) in 118 seconds. According to the *Guinness Book of Records*, it's the world's tallest outdoor elevator.
www.zhangjiajie.com.cn

🕂 2H ✉ Park entrance is 30km (18.5 miles) from Zhangjiajie City ☎ (0744) 571 2595 🚌 Minibuses from Zhangjiajie City 🚆 Zhangjiajie City has services to Changsha and Yichang 🖐 Expensive

HOTELS

GUANGZHOU
Shamian Hotel ($)
Situated on the south of Guangzhou's delightful Shamian Island, this is a good value, safe and clean budget option.

✉ 52 Shamiannan Jie ☎ (020) 8121 8359/8288

White Swan Hotel (Baitian'e Binguan) ($$$)
With a perfect view of the Pearl River this is arguably the best hotel in town, despite it also being Guangzhou's oldest five-star. Superb facilities include two swimming pools, fitness centre, indoor and outdoor tennis courts and a number of fine restaurants.

✉ 1 Shamian Nanjie, Shamian Island ☎ (020) 8188 6968; www.whiteswanhotel.com

GUILIN
Hotel of Modern Art (HOMA) ($$)
Extraordinary pyramid-shaped hotel located within the grounds of Yuzi Paradise, China's first dedicated to modern art. The expansive estate is surrounded by limestone karst peaks and contain more than 200 sculptures by international artists.

✉ Dabu Town, Yanshan District, Guilin (halfway between Guilin and Yangshuo) ☎ (0773) 386 5555; www.guilinhoma.com

HONG KONG
Alisan Guesthouse ($)
For cheaper, decent rooms Hong Kong Island-side, turn to this small and friendly Causeway Bay guesthouse.

✉ Flat A, 5th floor, Hoito Court, 23 Cannon Street, Causeway Bay
☎ (852) 2838 0762

Hong Kong Hostel ($)
HK Hostel may be cheap but in terms of location it's unparalleled. Located in a residential block bang in the middle of Causeway Bay, the HK Hostel offers modest home comforts in clean rooms.

✉ 3rd Floor, Block A, 47 Paterson Street, Causeway Bay ☎ (852) 2392 6868; www.hostel.hk

Landmark Mandarin Oriental ($$$)

This chic hotel is connected to the fashionable Landmark shopping mall. Flatscreen TVs are built into the bathroom's crescent-shaped wall and a socket conects your iPod to the stereo system.

✉ 15 Queen's Road, Central ☎ (852) 2132 0188; www.mandarinoriental.com

Peninsula Hong Kong ($$$)

See page 52.

MACAU
Pousada de Sao Tiago ($$$)

See page 52.

ZHANGJIAJIE
Xiangdian International Hotel ($$)

Rooms are based around peaceful courtyards and the glass-domed roof of the restaurant has views of the mountain peaks.

✉ Zhangjiajie Forest Park, Zhangjiajie ☎ (0744) 571 2999; www.xiangdianhotel.com

RESTAURANTS

GUANGZHOU
1920 Restaurant & Bar ($)

This riverfront German bar has a meaty menu and lashings of beer. It is popular with foreign visitors in town.

✉ 183 Yanjiangxi Lu, Guangzhou ☎ (020) 8333 6156 🕓 Daily 11am–late

Banxi Jiujia ($$)

Historic restaurant that remains popular for its dim sum delicacies and other Cantonese favourites.

✉ 151 Longjinxi Lu ☎ (020) 8172 1328 🕓 Daily breakfast, lunch and dinner

Guangzhou Restaurant ($$)

A local favourite, this old eatery specializes in seafood and the Cantonese dim sum.

✉ 2 Wenchangnan Lu ☎ (020) 8138 08083 🕓 Daily breakfast, lunch and dinner

Lotus Restaurant ($$)

Excellent dim sum restaurant serving Cantonese snacks and noodles from pushcarts.

✉ 67 Dishipu Lu ☎ (020) 8181 3388 🕐 Daily breakfast, lunch and dinner

HONG KONG
Aqua Roma & Aqua Tokyo ($$$)

Located on the top floor of TST's tallest harbour-front tower, Aqua Roma (Italian) has a floor-to-ceiling arched glass facade facing the harbour while Aqua Tokyo (Japanese) looks out over Kowloon's glittering urban cityscape. The Aqua Spirit cocktail bar is located just above on the mezzanine floor.

✉ 29th Fl, 1 Peking Road, Tsim Sha Tsui, Hong Kong ☎ (852) 3427 2288; www.aqua.com.hk 🕐 Daily lunch and dinner

Felix ($$$)

Felix has an incredible location on the 28th floor of the Peninsula Hong Kong Hotel (➤ 157). The restaurant serves a mix of European and Asian dishes.

✉ The Peninsula, Salisbury Road, Tsim Sha Tsui ☎ (852) 2315 3188; www.hongkong.peninsula.com 🕐 Daily lunch and dinner

Hutong ($$$)

Excellent Chinese food – with considerable spice and non-Cantonese flavour – is accompanied by staggering views. There is a lovely, traditionally inspired interior.

✉ 28th floor, 1 Peking Road, Tsim Sha Tsui, Kowloon ☎ (852) 3428 8342 🕐 Daily lunch and dinner

Tai Ping Koon ($)

Tai Ping Koon has been around since 1860 and is the pick of Causeway Bay's famed "soy sauce restaurants". These places dress Western food up in a quintessentially Cantonese way, to produce the sort of Chinese food that Europeans and Americans are used to.

✉ 6 Pak Sha Road, Causeway Bay ☎ (852) 2576 9161 🕐 Daily lunch and dinner

Tang Court ($$$)

With two Michelin stars, Tang Court takes its name from the Tang dynasty, with superb Cantonese food and elegant presentation.

✉ Langham Hotel, 8 Peking Road, Tsim Sha Tsui, Kowloon ☎ (852) 2375 1133 🕓 Mon–Fri 12–3, 6–11, Sat–Sun 11–3, 6–11

MACAU
Restaurante Fernando ($)

Breezy, seaside Fernando's has been serving fantastic seafood dishes for years from its location on the lovely island of Coloane.

✉ 9 Praia de Hac Sa, Coloane ☎ (853) 2888 2264; www.fernando-restaurant.com 🕓 Daily 12–9:30

XIAMEN
Gulang Xinyu Restaurant (Gulangyu Island) ($$$)

Excellent fresh seafood dishes are served in this restaurant on a lovely, car-free island.

✉ 4 Zhonghua Lu ☎ (0592) 206 3073 🕓 Daily lunch and dinner

YANGSHUO
Pure Lotus Vegetarian Restaurant ($$)

Well-presented meat-free dishes with a Buddhist slant, are served in this restaurant, tucked away from the noisy Yangshuo action.

✉ Diecui Lu ☎ (0773) 881 8995 🕓 Daily lunch and dinner

Le Votre ($$)

In a wooden dining hall, Le Votre specializes in French food but runs a sideline in deep fried snake, among other tasty local treats.

✉ 79 West Street, Yangshuo ☎ (0773) 882 8040 🕓 Daily lunch and dinner

SHOPPING

ARTS AND CRAFTS
Amazing Grace Elephant Company

A multitude of arts and crafts from all over East Asia. A great place to find unusual gifts.

✉ Star House, 5C1, Ground Floor, Harbour City, Kowloon, Hong Kong
☎ (852) 2730 5455

Eastern Dreams
Reproduction furniture and screens can be found here. There are also ceramics and woodcarvings.
✉ 47A Hollywood Road, Central, Hong Kong ☎ (852) 2544 2804

BOOKS
Page One
This is a huge English-language bookshop, reputedly the best in Hong Kong.
✉ Times Square, 1 Matheson Street, Causeway Bay, Hong Kong
☎ (852) 2506 0383

DEPARTMENT STORES
Festival Walk
Festival Walk has the largest book shop and cinema in town and a huge ice rink too.
✉ 80–88 Tat Chee Avenue, Kowloon, Hong Kong ☎ (852) 2844 2222;
www.festivalwalk.com.hk ◷ 10am–midnight

Harbour City
This goliath shopping complex comprises most of the western fringe of the Kowloon Peninsula and has four well-packed storeys.
✉ 3–9 Canton Road, Kowloon, Hong Kong ☎ (852) 2118 8666;
www.harbourcity.com.hk ◷ 10–9

IFC Mall
Strung between the two huge International Finance Center (IFC) towers, this mall is spacious and contains every major chain store.
✉ 8 Finance Street, Central, Hong Kong ☎ (852) 2295 3308;
www.ifc.com.hk ◷ 10:30–10

The Landmark
Hong Kong's most fashionable mall now houses nothing but five-star brands from all the big names in luxury retail. It also has the first Asian branch of London department store Harvey Nichols.
✉ 12–16 Des Voeux Road, Central, Hong Kong ☎ (852) 2525 4142;
www.centralhk.com ◷ 10:30–7:30

Langham Place

With around 300 stores spread over 15 storeys, this building is at the heart of an attempt to rejuvenate down-at-heel Mongkok.

✉ 8 Argyle Street, Mongkok, Hong Kong ☎ (852) 3520 2800; www.langhamplace.com.hk ◷ 10:30am–11pm

Pacific Place

One of the most democratic of Hong Kong Island's malls, Pacific Place has a variety of indie stores.

✉ 88 Queensway, Admiralty, Hong Kong ☎ (852) 2844 8988; www.pacificplace.co.hk ◷ 10:30am–11pm

Times Square

Times Square's twin towers rise to 46 and 39 storeys, the bottom 16 of which house a combination of international chains and local dealers, plus four storeys of restaurants and a cinema complex.

✉ 1 Matheson Street, Causeway Bay, Hong Kong ☎ (852) 2118 8900; www.timessquare.com.hk ◷ 10–10

ENTERTAINMENT

ARTS

Hong Kong Arts Centre

The arts centre contains galleries with exhibitions of contemporary art and also hosts a busy schedule of film and the performing arts.

✉ 2 Harbour Road, Wanchai, Hong Kong ☎ (852) 2582 0200; www.hkac.org.hk

Hong Kong Cultural Centre

The Cultural Centre is the home of the Hong Kong Philharmonic Orchestra – one of the best orchestras in the world.

✉ 10 Salisbury Road, Tsim Sha Tsui, Hong Kong ☎ (852) 2734 9011; www.lcsd.gov.hk/hkcc

Wanch

This long-standing Wan Chai spot has live rock and guitar music pretty much every night.

✉ 54 Jaffe Road, Wan Chai ☎ (852) 2861 1621 ◷ Daily 4pm–late

COOKING
Yangshuo Cooking School
Half-day lessons in a village farmhouse begin with students shopping in a local market and then being taught to cook five specific dishes. You get to keep the recipes.

✉ Chaolong Village, Yangshuo, Guangxi province ☎ (137) 8843 7286
🕓 9:30am (also 3:30pm start, Mar–Nov) 💰 Expensive

OUTDOOR SHOWS
Symphony of Lights
Twenty of Hong Kong Island's tallest buildings become a canvas to a series of synchronized searchlights and lasers in this nightly display. The show begins at 8pm and last around 20 minutes. The Tsim Sha Tsui Promenade at the southern tip of Kowloon offers uninterrupted views.

Impressions Liu Sanjie
A cast of 600 perform elegant routines on a floating set at the confluence of the Li and Yulong rivers. The backdrop is 12 karst limestone peaks, lit dramatically by spotlights.

✉ Li River Mountain-Water Theatre, Yangshuo ☎ (0773) 881 1982; www.yxlsj.com 🕓 Daily 7:40–8:50pm 💰 Expensive (from 188RMB)

SPORT

Hong Kong Horse Racing
Race meetings are held at Shatin in the New Territories most weekends during the season. The claustrophobic course at Happy Valley on Hong Kong Island has meetings most Wednesdays.

☎ www.hkjc.com 🕓 Sep–Jun 💰 Inexpensive

Macau Tower
This tower, 338m (1,110ft) tall, has a variety of thrilling rides and activities. The Mast Climb, Bungee Jump, SkyJump and Skywalk X all require a strong stomach.

✉ Largo da Torre de Macau, Hong Kong ☎ (853) 2893 3339; www.macautower.com.mo 🕓 Mon–Fri 10–9, Sat–Sun 9–9
💰 Moderate–expensive

Western China

The western half of China is a remarkably diverse region, stretching from the steamy jungles of Yunnan, close to the Burmese border, all the way to the deserts of Xinjiang, via the snow-capped peaks of Tibet and Sichuan. Compared with the densely populated eastern half of the country, the west is wild, frequently mountainous and often poor.

Chengdu

The culture is as varied as the topography. A rich Buddhist and Muslim heritage can be found in Gansu and Xinjiang provinces, where you can visit oasis cities along the ancient Silk Road, a route once travelled by camel caravans carrying goods between China and the mysterious western world. Known as the "Roof of the World", Tibet is located on the vast, windswept Qinghai-Tibet Plateau, and at an average 4,060m (13,321ft) above sea level. Tibet's magnificent Buddhist monasteries and unique Buddhist heritage are well worth exploring.

CHONGQING

One of China's most rapidly developing cities and gateway to the Three Gorges (➤ 40–41), Chongqing is one of the best places to observe the contrasts of modern China. As the economic powerhouse of the southwest, the city absorbs millions of migrants who spend their nights in the ghoulish grey tenement blocks and their days building towering skyscrapers. The city has a 2,000 year history and was the capital of the ancient state of Ba in the Zhou dynasty. Named an open treaty port in 1890, Chongqing attracted little foreign attention. Hongyan Cun, or **Red Crag Village**, served as the offices and residences for the Communist representatives during the war against the Japanese and a museum now stands on the site. The city centre has been built into the steep hillsides around two huge waterways – the Yangtze

and the Jialing. Two cableways connect the riverbanks and offer views of the downtown high-rises. With Chongqing's famously bad weather, it's a trip best made at night. Evening river cruises are also very popular, leaving from the dock at Chaotianmen. For a sense of history, visit the attractive and fascinating **Huguang Guildhall,** where opera performances are held twice a week. Chongqing is known as one of China's four "furnaces" due to the stifling heat in summer. Avoid travel during this time if possible.

✚ 1H ✉ Chongqing Municipality, 300km (186 miles) southeast of Chengdu 🚌 Express buses to Chengdu, Dazu, Leshan 🚆 Daily from Chengdu, Beijing, Dazu, Kunming, Shanghai ✈ Jiangbei International Airport

Red Crag Village

✉ Hongyan Lu ☎ (023) 6330 0192 🕐 Daily 8.30–5 👋 Inexpensive 🚌 104 on Beiqu Lu

Huguang Guildhall

✉ Dongshuimen Zhengjie ☎ (023) 6393 0287 🕐 Daily 9–6 👋 Inexpensive

DAZU

The Dazu Buddhist Caves, 160km (100 miles) northwest of Chongqing, are divided among 40 different locations, and include more than 50,000 carvings from the Tang and Song dynasties. This is one of the most important Buddhist archaeological sites in China, predating other such sites by hundreds of years. The two most popular caves are found at Beishan and Baodingshan, each of which contains around 10,000 sculptures.

The sculptures in **Baodingshan,** 15km (9 miles) northeast of Dazu, are said to be the most beautiful. Made during the Southern Song Dynasty, they are scattered around 13 different sites. The sculptures were paid for with funds raised by Zhao Zhifeng, a monk who turned Baodingshan into a centre of Tantric Buddhism. Cave 8 is home to the largest 1,000-armed Guanyin in China, with an eye in each of her palms. The Great Buddha Crescent is the site of the most famous Buddha at Dazu, the Reclining Buddha entering Nirvana, which stretches 31m (102ft) from head to knees.

Its sculptures carved in the Tang dynasty, **Beishan,** just 2km (1.25 miles) north of Dazu, has 290 caves. The sculptures here were produced in the Tang Dynasty. This was a former military stronghold held by Wei Junjing, a Sichuan military leader who ordered the construction of the first Buddhist temple at Beishan. Cave 136, the best preserved and largest of the caves, shows Puxian, the patron deity of Mount Emei, riding a white elephant, and Guanyin, the Goddess of Mercy. Also depicted is a large carved wheel representing the cycle of life and death, while a pagoda sits on the top of the mountain.

✚ 14R ⊠ 160km (100 miles) northwest of Chongqing, Chongqing Municipality 🍴 Street foodstalls on Shizi Jie 🚌 Daily to Chengdu, Chongqing

Baodingshan
⊠ Baoding Zhen 🕐 Daily 8–5 🖐 Moderate 🚌 Take a long-distance bus from Chongqing

Beishan
⊠ Baoding Zhen, Beishan 🕐 Daily 8–5 🖐 Moderate 🚌 Take a long-distance bus from Chongqing

Gansu and Qinghai Provinces

MOGAO KU (MOGAO CAVES)

Best places to see, ➤ 50–51.

QINGHAI HU (QINGHAI LAKE)

Qinghai Lake is a salt water lake in northeast Qinghai Province,
300km (186 miles) from Xining. It is the largest inland lake in
China, covering an area of 4,455sq km (1,720sq miles) and with a
circumference of 900km (560 miles). The name of the province –
Qinghai (which literally means Blue Sea) – comes from this huge
body of water (which in Chinese is referred to as a "sea" rather
than a "lake"). Called the Western Sea in ancient times, the lake
was formed around a million years ago. Qinghai Lake is
surrounded by mountains, and more than 50 rivers run into it. It's
drained by the Yellow River and its tributaries. Bird Island, located
on the western side of the lake, is the largest breeding ground for
birds in China, with some 12 species migrating here from India and
southern China to breed from March to early June. Birds found
here include wild geese, gulls, cormorants, sandpipers, and the
rare black-necked cranes.

✚ 12Q ✉ 155km (96 miles) from Xining, Qinghai Province 🚌 Regular buses
from Xining to Heimahe ❓ Tours to Bird Island can be booked in Xining

Sichuan Province

CHANG JIANG (YANGTZE RIVER)

Best places to see, ➤ 40–41.

CHENGDU

The capital of Sichuan Province is one of China's fastest growing cities, combining modern, broad, tree-lined avenues with older areas of traditional, half-timbered houses. One such traditional house is **Du Fu's Thatched Cottage.** Du Fu (712–770), one of China's greatest poets, retired here in 759, writing 240 poems during his three-year stay. In the Song Dynasty, a thatched cottage was erected on the site of the original cottage. The thatched

cottage was later expanded to include a garden, making it a pleasant place for a stroll.

The **Wenshu Yuan** temple was founded in the 6th century and is the headquarters of Zen (Chan) Buddhism in China. The temple, which is dedicated to the God of Wisdom, was destroyed in fighting during the Ming Dynasty, and rebuilt in 1691. The bustling street in front of the temple is also worth visiting, with peddlers selling incense, candles, prayer beads and ghost money. Also worth visiting is **Wuhouci** (Wuhou Temple), a series of memorial halls dedicated to Zhu Geliang, a military hero from Chinese lore. The temple was founded in the fifth century, but was rebuilt in 1672, and was recently restored.

Sichuan is the home of China's lovable Giant Panda and around 10km (6 miles) north of Chengdu is the **Giant Panda Breeding Base**. The centre's breeding success means you'll likely be able to view new born clubs with their mothers, especially in the autumn.

When you have finished sightseeing in town, turn to Sichuan province's most famous export (after its panda bears): its fiery food. The most famous of China's spicy cooking schools, Sichuan food is celebrated for its use of a herb called huajiao which numbs the mouth. Combined with chilli peppers, the result is delicious and can be experienced across Chengdu.

✚ 13R ✉ Capital of Sichuan Province ▣ Express buses to Chongqing, Leshan ▣ Daily from Chongqing, Beijing, Guangzhou, Kunming, Shanghai, Xi'an ✖ Shangliu Airport

Du Fu's Thatched Cottage

✉ 38 Qinghai Lu ☎ www.dfmuseum.org.cn 🕓 Daily 8–6:30 ▣ 301

Wenshu Yuan (Manjusiri Temple)

✉ 3 Duan Renmin Zhonglu 🕓 Daily 6am–9pm 🖐 Inexpensive ▣ 55, 64

Wuhouci (Wuhou Temple)

✉ 231 Wuhouci Dajie 🕓 Daily 8–6 ▣ 1, 57, 59, 334

Giant Panda Breeding Base

✉ 26 Xiongmao Dadao, Futoushan ☎ (028) 8351 6748; www.panda.org.cn 🕓 Daily 7–6 🖐 Moderate

EMEISHAN (MT EMEI)

One of China's four sacred Buddhist Mountains, Emeishan represents Puxian, the Bodhisattva of Universal Kindness, usually seen riding a white elephant. Emeishan is covered with bamboo, fir trees, pine trees and a variety of plants and flowers, and has a wide variety of butterflies, birds, monkeys, and even pandas on its more remote slopes. There are two trails up the mountain, which at 3,000m (9,483ft), is a tough climb. The northern route is shorter and more direct. There are about 30 temples on the mountain, the most famous of which is Baoguo Temple, considered the gateway to Emeishan. The walk up and down the mountain can take two to four days, but there are hostels along the way to break up the trip. For those seeking an easier route there are buses running to a point half way up, where you can transfer to a cable car after a short walk.

✚ 13R ✉ 6.5km (4 miles) west of Emei Town, 35km (22 miles) west of Leshan, Sichuan Province ☎ (0833) 559 0111; www.ems517.com ⏰ 24 hours 🚌 Regular buses between Emei Town and Leshan and Chengdu 🚆 Daily from Chengdu, Kunming ✋ Expensive

JIUZHAIGOU NATIONAL PARK

Tucked away in the mountains of northern Sichuan, Jiuzhaigou is a series of three interconnected valleys which have colourful forest canopies, gushing waterfalls and aquamarine lakes, all framed against a snowy mountain backdrop. The Chinese name translates as "nine village valley", referring to the original Tibetan settlements that dotted the landscape. Though there are still a few prayer wheels and Tibetan stupa, the three remaining villages have lost much of their appeal and can hardly be described as attractions in their own right. The main motivation for modern visitors is the spectacular alpine scenery. It's more than 30km (18.5 miles) from the entrance, in the north, to the most southerly extremity of the park which lies 3,060m (10,040ft) above sea-level. Shuttle buses whisk travellers around and set off every ten minutes.

www.jiuzhai.com
🔳 13R 📮 Jiuzhaigou County, 435km north of Chengdu
☎ (0837) 773 9753; 🕓 1 Apr–15 Nov 7am–7:30pm; 16 Nov–31 Mar 8–5:30 🚌 Daily departures for Chengdu 💵 Expensive
✈ Jiuzhaigou Huanglong Airport; daily flights to Chengdu

LESHAN

Carved in the face of a cliff in the Tang Dynasty, Leshan's Maitreya Buddha gazes calmly over the confluence of the Min, Dadu and Qingyi rivers.

The statue is the largest carved stone Buddha in the world. It is known in Chinese simply as Dafo, or the Big Buddha. The seated statue is 71m (232ft) tall. The head alone is 14.7m (48ft), the ears 7m (23ft) long. The statue can be viewed by boat from the river, or by climbing to the top of the hill next to where the statue stands and then descending the steps to its foot.

www.leshandafo.com

🔳 13R 📮 115km (71 miles) south of Chengdu, Sichuan Province ☎ (0833) 230 2416; 🕓 Apr–7 Oct daily 7:30–6:30; 8 Oct–Mar 8–5:30 🚌 Regular buses to Chengdu. From Leshan city, take bus 3 or 13 to the park gate 💵 Moderate 🚤 Tour boats leave Leshan pier every 30 min, daily 7–5

Tibet Autonomous Region

Tibetan culture prospered during the 10th to the 16th centuries. In
the 18th century China made Tibet a protectorate, and began to
control the Dalai Lamas. Tibet became relatively independent after
the 1911 revolution, but was seized by China in 1950. The region
remains restive: anti-Chinese riots in March 2008 led to a number
of deaths and Tibet remains periodically inaccessible to foreign
visitors, so check before planning a trip.

GANDEN GOMPA (GANDEN MONASTERY)

Ganden Monastery, built in the early 15th century by Tsongkhapa,
is today home to several hundred Buddhist monks. The monastery
was seriously damaged during the Cultural Revolution. A stupa at
the monastery holds the remains of Tsongkhapa, founder of the
Yellow Hat Sect of Tibbetan Buddhism.

✚ 10R ✉ 45km (28 miles) east of Lhasa ⏱ Daily dawn–dusk ✋ Moderate

GYANTSE

Travellers to Shigatse often stop off at Gyantse, situated at the
juncture of two important caravan routes to India and Nepal.

The city, Tibet's fourth largest, was important strategically, and was once a major trading centre for nomads. The **Palkhor Monastery,** built in the 1427, has been badly damaged, but is worth visiting, especially its Nepalese Kumbun stupa with painted eyes and beautiful murals. The city's old fort, or Dzong, was hit by British artillery in 1904 and again by the People's Liberation Army in 1960.

🚽 10R ✉ 255km (158 miles) southwest of Lhasa, Tibet 🚌 Minibuses from Lhasa via Shigatse

Palkhor Monastery

✉ Gyantse 🕐 Daily 9–6 ✋ Moderate

LHASA

Best places to see, ➤ 46–47.

SAMYE

Samye Monastery, the first Buddhist monastery to be built in Tibet, was founded by an Indian scholar, the abbot Shantarakshita, during the reign of King Trisong Detsen in the eighth century.

🚽 10R ✉ Approximately 30km (19 miles) west of Tsetang 🕐 Daily 8–6 ✋ Inexpensive

SHIGATSE

In the valley of the Yarlong Tsangpo River (the Brahmaputra in India), Shigatse is Tibet's second-largest urban area. The city was dominated by the Red Hat Sect until the fifth Dalai Lama defeated the sect with the support of the Mongolians, uniting the country under the Yellow Hat Sect. The beautiful Tashilhunpo Monastery, the seat of the Panchen Lama, was built here in 1447. The monastery, terraced on a hillside, has a 28m (92ft) statue of the Maitreya Buddha and a Grand Hall that houses the tomb of the fourth Panchen Lama.

🚽 9R ✉ 250km (155 miles) southwest of Lhasa 🚌 Minibuses from Lhasa

Yunnan Province

DALI

The old walled town of Dali sits on the
edge of Erhai Lake, with the Azure
(Cangshan) Mountains a beautiful backdrop.
The main ethnic group is the Bai, believed
to have built settlements here 3,000 years
ago, and known for their colourful dress
and embroidery. The Bai defeated Tang
troops in the eighth century to establish the
Nanzhao Kingdom which, at its height,
spread to parts of Burma and Laos.
Nanzhao, later renamed Dali, remained
independent until 1253, when it was
conquered by the Mongols led by Kublai
Khan, who made it part of his empire.

The main street, Huguo Lu, is lined with
restaurants and shops selling embroidery,
batiks and marble. **The Three Pagodas,**
northwest of the city, were built during the
Tang Dynasty. The restored Chongsheng
Temple, behind the three pagodas, is a

good example of the traditional temple architecture of Yunnan Province.

🚇 12T 📮 300km (186 miles) west of Kunming, Yunnan Province 🍴 Restaurants along Boai Lu and Huguo Lu 🚌 Buses from Xiaguan, Lijiang and Kunming ✈ Xiaguan Airport (45 min from Dali)

The Three Pagodas

📮 2km (1 mile) northwest of Dali 🕐 Daily 7–7 ✋ Moderate

LIJIANG

Best places to see, ➤ 48–49.

XISHUANGBANNA

Located in a subtropical region in southwest Yunnan Province, Xishuangbanna borders Burma and Laos. According to the indigenous Dai people, Xishuangbanna was discovered thousands of years ago by hunters chasing golden deer. When the Mongols invaded China in the 13th century, the Dai fled south to this area, which was soon made part of the Chinese empire. Despite this, they managed to retain their own language and customs. Jinghong, the capital of the Xishuangbanna Dai Autonomous Prefecture, is a jumping off point for trips to surrounding stilt villages. The most important annual event is the Water Splashing Festival in mid-April, a celebration of the Dai New Year.

🚇 12T 📮 Southern Yunnan Province 🚌 Buses from Kunming to Jinghong ✈ Jinghong International Airport (5km/3 miles south of town). Daily flights to Kunming; peak season flights to Dali and Lijiang ❓ Water Splashing Festival, 13–15 Apr

Xinjiang Autonomous Region

The Xinjiang Uighur Autonomous Region is the largest province in China. The population is primarily made up of Arabic, Turkic-speaking peoples of Central Asian extraction and Han Chinese settlers. Like Tibet, some of the indigenous inhabitants chafe under Han control of the region and vicious riots in 2009 in the regional capital Urumqi led to a large number of deaths.

KASHGAR

Kashgar, located in the far west of Xinjiang towards the border with Pakistan, is the westernmost town in China. The city, which opened to visitors in 1985, remains primarily Central Asian, with little Chinese flavour.

In ancient times, Kashgar was one of the most important oasis towns on the Silk Road between the Middle East and China. The 1986 opening of the Karakorum Highway, linking China and Pakistan, bolstered the city's position as a significant transport hub.

Some 150,000 people visit the Sunday Market, just 2km (1.25 miles) from the centre of town, each week to purchase metal ware, jewellery, rugs, pottery, musical instruments and spices as well as to sample traditional Central Asian specialities, such as naan bread and mutton kebabs.

Centrally located, the **Id Kah Mosque** is one of the largest mosques in China. It is believed to have been built in 1738 but has been renovated several times since. The mosque's main hall can accommodate about 20,000 worshippers.

In an eastern suburb of Kashgar stands the imposing
Mausoleum of Abakh Khoja – a 17th-century Muslim holy man
– and five generations of his family. This elegant domed structure
is also said to be the burial place of Xiangfei, a beautiful
concubine of the Qing Emperor Qianlong, believed to be Abakh
Khoja's daughter.

➕ 7N ✉ Xinjiang Province, about 1,500km (932 miles) west of Urumqi
🍴 Uighur foodstalls outside the Id Kah Mosque 🚌 Buses to Kyrgyzstan,
Pakistan and Urumqi 🚉 Daily from Urumqi ✈ Kashgar Airport (12km/7.5
miles northeast of town, but very few flights)

Id Kah Mosque
✉ Jiefang Beilu, west of Id Kah Square ☎ (0998) 282 7113 🕐 Daily 9–7
✋ Inexpensive

Mausoleum of Abakh Hoja
✉ Aizilaiti Lu ☎ (0998) 265 0630 🕐 Daily 10–dusk ✋ Inexpensive

TURPAN (TURFAN OR TULUFAN)

Once a major oasis town on the Silk Road between China and the Middle East, Turpan was also an important Buddhist centre, until migrations of Uighurs brought the area under the influence of Islam in the eighth century. Turpan is today an agricultural centre famous for sweet Hami melons, dates and grapes. The city is also known as the Land of Fire, due to its intense summer heat, which can exceed 47°C (116°F). Many famous 20th-century Western explorers and archaeologists came here to explore the nearby caves and shipped crates of sculptures, frescoes and other treasures and artefacts to Europe. The city has a busy Sunday bazaar, where colourful silk dresses and hats are a speciality. The circular Emin Minaret, at the Suleiman Mosque, was built in 1777 using unglazed mud bricks.

Bezeklik, located in the mountains outside the city, is a Buddhist cave with deteriorated carvings made between the fifth and 14th centuries. The ancient desert ruins of Jiaohe and Gaochang are a short drive out of town. Also nearby are the Flaming Mountains, so named because of their deep red hue.

🚩 10N ⊠ 165km (103 miles) east of Urumqi, Xinjiang Province 🚌 Buses to Urumqi, minibuses to Daheyan 🚉 Daheyan Station 58km (36 miles) north of Turpan

Bezeklik

⊠ Northwest of the Flaming Mountains 🕐 Daily 9–5 💷 Moderate

HOTELS

CHENGDU
Crowne Plaza Chengdu ($$$)
The top hotel in Chengdu and situated in the heart of the city. Great restaurants and fitness facilities, and the popular Rainbow Crowne Nite Club is busy most nights.

✉ 31 Zhongfu Lu ☎ (028) 8678 6666; www.ichotelsgroup.com

Traffic Inn ($)
Excellent hostel with some great, good-value doubles and dorms next to its namesake hotel on Linjiang Lu by the river. There are English-speaking staff.

✉ 6 Linjiang Lu ☎ (028) 8545 0470

CHONGQING
Hilton Chongqing ($$)
The Hilton Chongqing offers a slice of Shanghai class in the midst of the Chinese hinterland, with spacious rooms (some with views of the river) and a range of top-notch restaurants.

✉ 139 Zhongshan Sanlu ☎ (023) 8903 8558; www.hilton.com

Wudu Binguan ($$)
A standard, moderately priced hotel, the Wudu Binguan has a good French restaurant.

✉ 24 Shang Zhengjiayan, Zhongshansi Lu, Yuzhongqu ☎ (023) 6385 1788

DALI
Jim's Tibetan Hostel ($)
Jim's has lovely rooms and a great atmosphere, with a terrace and bar. This hostel is one of the best in town.

✉ 13 Yuxiu Lu ☎ (0872) 267 7824; jimstibetanhotel@gmail.com

Jinhua Hotel ($)
The Jinhua has a prime setting at the very heart of ancient Dali. All rooms provide cable television and the hotel has a friendly bar and lounge.

✉ Corner of Huguo Lu and Fuxing Jie ☎ (0872) 267 3343

DAZU
Dazu Hotel ($)
Best location for visiting Beishan and Baodingshan. Amenities include a fitness centre and an in-house nightclub.

✉ 47 Gongnong, Longgang Town ☎ (023) 4372 2250

DUNHUANG
Silk Road Dunhuang Hotel (Dunhuang Shanzhuang) ($$)
In the sand dunes south of town, the hotel provides every possible convenience including camel riding, sand sledding and archery.

✉ Dunyue Lu ☎ (0937) 888 2088; www.dunhuangresort.com

EMEISHAN
Jinding Hotel ($$)
Situated just below the summit of 3,099m (10,168ft), the Jinding is an ideal place for a rest after climbing the sacred Buddhist mountain or bedding down before a sunrise visit to the peak.

✉ Golden Summit, Emeishan ☎ (0833) 509 8088

JIUZHAIGOU
Resort Jiuzhai Paradise ($$)
Nestled against the snow-capped mountains of north Sichuan. The highlight is the reception – a gigantic glass dome bubble with rock pools, rivers and bars set within recreated traditional buildings.

✉ Ganhaizi, Zhangzha Town, Jiuzhaigou County ☎ (0837) 778 9999; www.ichotelsgroup.com

KASHGAR
Qianhai Hotel ($)
A quiet, laid-back place with a few facilities including a restaurant. The hotel is located west of the main square.

✉ 199 Renminxi Lu ☎ (0998) 283 1805

LHASA
Lhasa Hotel ($$)
The Lhasa is a comfortable three-star hotel with five restaurants, and satellite television in every room. This place has hot water all

year round, something that cannot be said for some of Lhasa's other hotels.

✉ 1 Minzu Lu ☎ (0891) 683 2221

House of Shambhala ($$)
Hailed as the first boutique hotel in Tibet, this 10-room property is set in a restored Tibetan courtyard home.

✉ 7 Jiri Erxiang (just south of Barkhor Square) ☎ (010) 6402 7151; www.shambhalaserai.com

Kyichu Hotel ($$)
This friendly, family-run lodge is one of Lhasa's oldest private hotels and remains one of the classiest accommodation options in town.

✉ 149 Beijing Donglu, Lhasa ☎ (0891) 633 1541; www.kyichuhotel.com

TURPAN
Oasis Hotel (Luzhou Binguan) ($)
Facilities at the Oasis include an Internet cafe and sauna room. The restaurant serves excellent regional specialities.

✉ 41 Qingnianbei Lu ☎ (0995) 852 2491

RESTAURANTS

CHENGDU
Baguo Buyi Restaurant ($$)
One of Chengdu's more fashionable restaurants, Baguo Buyi has several branches across China. This place specializes in traditionally spicy Sichuan fare. Ask after the "clothes hanger" dish which features thin strips of cucumber and pork slices hanging over a wooden railing.

✉ 8 Guangfuqiao Beijie ☎ (028) 8551 1999 🕐 Daily lunch and dinner

Bookworm ($)
This excellent cafe and bookshop has a great range of English books and a comfy ambience that draws in travellers.

✉ 28 Renmin Nanlu ☎ (028) 8552 0177; www.chengdubookworm.com
🕐 Daily 9am–late

Chen Mapo Doufu Restaurant ($)
See page 59.

Huangcheng Laoma Restaurant ($$)
Traditional Sichuan hotpot restaurant. Order meat and vegetables
and cook them in the hotpot at your own table.
✉ 106 Qintai Lu ☎ (028) 8613 1752 🕐 Daily lunch and dinner

Long Chaoshou ($–$$)
Opened in 1940, this is one of Chengdu's oldest and most famous
restaurants. The three floors serve different types of food.
✉ 48 South Chunxi Lu ☎ (028) 8666 6947 🕐 Daily breakfast, lunch and
dinner

Sultan ($)
If you've had one spicy Sichuan dish or hotpot too many, head to
this relaxing and very comfortable Turkish restaurant in the south
of town, much-loved for its kebabs and Middle Eastern flavours.
✉ 1 Yulin Nanjie ☎ 028) 8555 4780 🕐 Daily 11–11

DALI
Cafe de Jack ($)
This place has been going a reassuringly long time, offering a good
range of local dishes along with backpacker fare and an excellent
roof terrace.
✉ 82 Boai Lu ☎ (0872) 267 1572 🕐 Daily 8am–late

Sunshine Café ($)
Simple Western, Bai and Chinese fare served by friendly staff
in a laid-back setting. Hearty breakfasts are accompanied by
Yunnan coffee.
✉ 16 Huguo Lu ☎ (0872) 266 0712 🕐 Daily lunch and dinner

DUNHUANG
The excellent night market off Yangguan Donglu, nearly opposite
the Dunhuang Museum, has loads of stalls selling roast lamb and
noodles till late.

Charley Johng's Café ($)

Serves decent Chinese and Western food and staff can help to buy tickets. Bike rental and Internet also available.

✉ Mingshan Lu, opposite the stadium ☎ (0937) 883 3039 🕐 Daily breakfast, lunch and dinner

Shirley's Café ($)

Similiar to Charley Johng's (Shirley is said to be his sister). Food is rather simple, but the location is central.

✉ Mingshan Lu, opposite Charley Johng's Café ☎ (0937) 882 6387 🕐 Daily breakfast, lunch and dinner

EMEISHAN
Teddy Bear Café ($)

Popular with backpackers, this simple restaurant serves both Western and Sichuan dishes and does a good cup of coffee.

✉ 42 Baoguo Lu, on the road leading to Baoguo Monastery ☎ (0833) 559 0135; www.teddybear.com.cn 🕐 Daily breakfast, lunch and dinner

KASHGAR
John's Café ($)

This long-standing place, near the Seman Hotel in west Kashgar, is a handy pit stop for Western and Chinese meals and information.

✉ 337 Seman Lu ☎ (0998) 258 1186; www.johncafe.net 🕐 Daily 8am–midnight

LHASA
Lhasa Kitchen ($)

The Lhasa Kitchen has a great second-floor location nearby Jokhang Temple. It's popular with both the local monks and tourists and offers Western, Nepali and Indian cuisine.

✉ 3 Minchi Khang Donglu ☎ (0891) 634 8855) 🕐 Daily 8am–10pm

New Mandala Restaurant ($)

Tasty Nepalese dishes and a great location just west of the Jokhang Temple make this a popular spot for visitors to Lhasa.

✉ Zangyiyuan Lu ☎ (0891) 634 2235 🕐 Daily 8am–10pm

Norling Restaurant ($$)

The terrace and courtyard garden of the Kyichu Hotel are a good alfresco option. A wide variety of Tibetan, Nepali and Indian dishes is served.

✉ Kyichu Hotel, 18 Beijing Zhonglu ☎ (0891) 633 1541; www.kyichuhotel.com ⏰ Daily 7:30am–10pm

Snowlands Restaurant ($)

Inexpensive Chinese, Tibetan, Indian and Western dishes are served in an unpretentious setting.

✉ 4 Zangyiyuan Lu ☎ (0891) 633 7323 ⏰ Daily breakfast, lunch and dinner

URUMQI
Fubar ($)

This place is a welcoming spot for a beer, with a tasty menu of pub food.

✉ 40 Gongyuan Beijie ☎ (0991) 584 4498; www.fubarchina.com ⏰ Daily 11am–late

LIJIANG
Lamu's House of Tibet ($)

See page 59.

Mama Fu's ($)

Enjoy Chinese and Western dishes alfresco in a pleasant setting beside the canal.

✉ 76 Xinyi Jie, Mishi Xiang ☎ (0888) 512 2285 ⏰ Daily lunch and dinner

SHOPPING

CHENGDU
Shu Brocade Academy

Weavers use traditional wooden looms to make sumptuous silk brocade, which is one of Sichuan's most celebrated products. Next door is an embroidery shop and a factory which offers tours to visitors.

✉ 268 Huanhua Nanlu ☎ (028) 8738 3891 ⏰ Daily 8:30–6

DALI
Shaping Market
Village markets around Dali take place most days, including a Bai market on Mondays at Shaping around 30km (18 miles) north of town, full of ethnic Bai clothing, jewellery and more. Haggle hard.

✉ Shaping Market, Shaping ⏱ Mon 10am to mid-afternoon

LIJIANG
Bunong Bells
Sells engraved bronze bells, the like of which were used by itinerant traders along the old Yunnan-Tibet tea trading trail to attract local villagers.

✉ Dashi Qiao, Old Town ☎ (0888) 512 6638 ⏱ Daily 8:30am–1:30am

ENTERTAINMENT

ARTS
Naxi Orchestra
Tradtional Naxi and Chinese music is played on classical instruments by a white wispy bearded cohort under the direction of local legend Xuan Ke.

✉ Naxi Music Academy, Dong Dajie, Lijiang, Yunnan Province ☎ (0888) 512 7971 ⏱ Daily 8pm–10pm ✋ Expensive

MASSAGE
House of Shambhala Yoga-Spa Centre
Located within Lhasa's new boutique hotel, House of Shambhala hotel, this spa uses locally sourced products and oils.

✉ 7 Jiri Erxiang (just south of Barkhor Square), Lhasa, Tibet ☎ (010) 6402 7151 (Beijing office); www.houseofshambhala.com ✋ Expensive

SPORT

Shun Jiang Horse Trek Company
Offers guided treks up into the mountains that surround Songpan, close to Jiuzhaigou in northern Sichuan. A trek can cost as little as 200RMB per day, per person. It's well worth stopping in this beautiful mountain town on the way to Jiuzhaigou.

✉ Songpan, Sichuan Province ☎ (0837) 880 9118

Index

Acknowledgements

The Automobile Association would like to thank the following photographers, companies and picture libraries for their assistance in the preparation of this book.

Abbreviations for the picture credits are as follows – (t) top; (b) bottom; (c) centre; (l) left; (r) right; (AA) AA World Travel Library.

4l Summer Palace AA/A Mockford & N Bonetti; **4c** Beijing airport AA/A Mockford & N Bonetti; **4r** Moon Hill, Yangshuo AA/ D Henley; **5l** Erhai Lake, Dali AA/D Henley; **5c** Brushes AA/B Madison; **6/7** Summer Palace AA/A Mockford & N Bonetti; **8/9** Shanghai AA/A Mockford & N Bonetti; **10tr** Hall of Jade Ripples, Summer Palace AA/A Mockford & N Bonetti; **10cr** Temple of the Town Gods, Shanghai AA/G Clements; **10bl** Emperor's hat, AA/A Mockford & N Bonetti; **10/11** Temple of Heaven, Beijing AA/A Mockford & N Bonetti; **11tr** Yu Gardens, Shanghai AA/A Mockford & N Bonetti; **11br** Guilin AA/D Henley; **12tr** Food stall AA/G Clements; **12bl** Fortune cookie Photodisc; **12/13** Sanlitun Lu street, Beijing AA/A Mockford & N Bonetti; **13tl** TMSK Crystal Bar, Shanghai AA/A Mockford & N Bonetti; **13tr** Chopsticks Stockbyte Royalty Free; **13bl** Teashop, Houhai Lake, Beijing AA/A Mockford & N Bonetti; **14t** Pickles AA/G Clements; **14b** Beer AA/D Henley; **15l** Tea cup, AA/A Mockford & N Bonetti; **15r** Chillis AA/B Madison; **16** Tiantan Park, Beijing; **16/17** Dried produce AA/D Henley; **17** Commuters AA/T Kaewdungdee; **18t** Tiananmen Square AA/A Mockford & N Bonetti; **18b** Peking duck AA/A Mockford & N Bonetti; **19** Tea house, Gu Shan island, Hangzhou; **20/21** Beijing airport AA/A Mockford & N Bonetti; **25** New Year, Yunnan AA/I Morejohn; **26** Shanghai airport AA/A Mockford & N Bonetti; **28/29** Xi'an AA/B Madison; **34/35** Moon Hill, Yangshuo AA/D Henley; **36** Terracotta warrior AA/B Madison; **36/37t** Terracotta warriors in rows AA/B Madison; **36/37b** Museum of Terracotta Warriors AA/B Madison; **38** Great Wall of China at Simatai AA/A Mockford & N Bonetti; **38/39** Great Wall of China at Simatai AA/G Clements; **39** Great Wall at Jiayuguan AA/I Morejohn; **40** Near Qutang Gorge AA/D Henley; **40/41** Ferry leaving Chongqing AA/A Kouprianoff; **42cr** Palace of Heavenly Purity AA/A Mockford & N Bonetti; **42b** Nine Dragons Screen AA/A Mockford & N Bonetti; **43** Cauldron AA/A Mockford & N Bonetti; **44** Lamma Island AA/B Bachman; **44/45t** View from The Peak AA/N Hicks; **44/45c** Man Mo Temple AA/N Hicks; **46** Man with prayer wheel AA/I Morejohn; **46/47** Potala Palace AA/I Morejohn; **47** National Grand Theatre, Photolibrary; **48/49** Naxi musicians AA/I Morejohn; **49** Black Dragon Pond with Jade Dragon Snow Mountain beyond AA/D Henley; **50** Exterior of the caves AA/D Henley; **51** Mogao Caves AA/D Henley; **52** Tsingtao and Yanjing beer AA/A Mockford & N Bonetti; **52/53** Former German Governor's residence AA/I Morejohn; **54** Yangshuo AA/D Henley; **54/55** Karst peaks AA/D Henley; **56/57** Erhai lake, Dali AA/D Henley; **58** Restaurant, AA/B. T. Madison; **59** Mantou, AA/A Mockford & N Bonetti; **60/61** Cyclists, AA/B. T. Madison; **62** Shopping at The Peninsula Hong Kong, © The Peninsula Hong Kong; **63** Felix, Restaurant, The Peninsula Hong Kong, © The Peninsula Hong Kong; **64/65** Star Ferry, AA/B Bachman; **67** Light of Wisdom hall, Shanghai Science and Technology Museum AA/A Mockford & N Bonetti; **69** Great Wall at Simitai AA/G Clements; **70/71** Brushes AA/B Madison; **73** Tiananmen Square AA/A Mockford & N Bonetti; **74** Gate of Supreme Harmony, Imperial Palace, AA/G. D. R. Clements; **75** White Cloud Temple AA/A Kouprianoff; **76/77** Beihai Park AA/A Kouprianoff; **76c** Green dragon tiles AA/A Mockford & N Bonetti; **77** National Grand Theatre, Photolibrary; **78** Incense sticks AA/A Mockford & N Bonetti; **78/79b** Confucius Temple AA/G Clements; **79cr** Revolutionary statue AA/A Mockford & N Bonetti; **79br** Mao's Mausoleum AA/A Mockford & N Bonetti; **80** Qianmen AA/G Clements; **81** Changling AA/I Morejohn; **82t** Gate Of Temple Of Heaven, Tai Miao, Photolibrary; **82b** Tiananmen Gate, Tiananmen Square, AA/A Mockford & N Bonetti; **83** Tiananmen Square AA/G Clements; **84tl** Hall of Prayer for Good Harvests AA/A Mockford & N Bonetti; Southern Cathedral interior AA/G Clements; **86/87** Garden of Harmonious Pleasure, Summer Palace AA/A Mockford & N Bonetti; **87** Kunming Lake, Summer Palace, Damian Harper; **88** Lama Temple AA/A Mockford & N Bonetti; **88/89** Ruins in the grounds of the Old Summer Palace AA/G Clements; **90tr** Gateway to Prince Gong's Mansion AA/A Mockford & N Bonetti; **90bl** Bar, Houhai Lake AA/A Mockford & N Bonetti; **91cl** Dog in basket AA/A Mockford & N Bonetti; **91br** Statue, Prince Gong's Mansion AA/A Mockford & N Bonetti; **92b** Puning Temple AA/D Henley; **92/93t** Locks placed by devotees AA/D Henley; **94t** Russian Matrioshka dolls AA/B Madison; **94/95c** St Sofia's Church AA/B Madison; **95** Drum Tower exterior, Xi'an AA/B Madison; **97** Drum Tower detail, Xi'an AA/B Madison; **98** Hanging Temple AA/I Morejohn; **98/99t** Woman harvesting grain AA/I Morejohn; **109** Humble Administrator's Garden, Suzhou AA/A Mockford & N Bonetti; **110/111** Huangpu River, Photolibrary; **112t** French Concession AA/A Mockford & N Bonetti; **112/113** Fuxing Park, French Concession AA/A Mockford & N Bonetti; **113** Nanjing Road AA/G Clements; **114** The Bund AA/A Mockford & N Bonetti; **115** Tai chi AA/G Clements; **116** Oriental Pearl TV Tower AA/A Mockford & N Bonetti; **117** Chinese Ethnic Minorities Arts and Crafts Gallery, Shanghai Museum AA/A Mockford & N Bonetti; **118** Shanghai Art Museum, AA/A Mockford & N Bonetti; **119** The Yard fashion store, Tianzifang Art Street, © TAO Images Limited/Alamy; **120** Yu Garden AA/G Clements; **121** Woman in Jade Buddha Temple AA/A Kouprianoff; **122** Longmen Caves, near Luoyang AA/I Morejohn; **122/123t** Huangshan AA/I Morejohn; **122/123b** The Pagoda Forest, Shaolin Temple AA/I Morejohn; **124** Monk AA/D Henley; **124/125** Stone camel statues near Ming Xiaoling AA/A Mockford & N Bonetti; **125** Humble Administrator's Garden, Suzhou AA/A Mockford & N Bonetti; **126/127** Taihan AA/I Morejohn; **127b** Miniature statues of Confucius AA/T Kaewdungdee; **128** West Lake AA/D Henley; **129** Tea House lantern AA/D Henley; **139** View from The Peak, Hong Kong AA/D Henley; **140/141t** Hong Kong Mueum of History, AA/B Bachman; **140/141b** Hong Kong island, Central District skyline, AA/B Bachman; **142tr** Po Lin Monastery AA/B Bachman; **142/143** Peak Tram AA/B Bachman;

Sight locator index

This index relates to the maps on the covers. We have given map references to the main sights of interest in the book. Grid references in italics indicate sights featured on town maps. Some sights within towns may not be plotted on the maps.

Dear Reader

Your comments, opinions and recommendations are very important to us. Please help us to improve our travel guides by taking a few minutes to complete this simple questionnaire.

You do not need a stamp (unless posted outside the UK). If you do not want to cut this page from your guide, then photocopy it or write your answers on a plain sheet of paper.

Send to: **The Editor, AA World Travel Guides, FREEPOST SCE 4598, Basingstoke RG21 4GY.**

Your recommendations...

We always encourage readers' recommendations for restaurants, nightlife or shopping – if your recommendation is used in the next edition of the guide, we will send you a **FREE AA Guide** of your choice from this series. Please state below the establishment name, location and your reasons for recommending it.

_____
_____
_____
_____
_____

Please send me **AA Guide** _____

About this guide...

Which title did you buy?

AA _____

Where did you buy it? _____

When? m m / y y

Why did you choose this guide? _____

_____
_____
_____
_____

Did this guide meet your expectations?

Exceeded ☐   Met all ☐   Met most ☐   Fell below ☐

Were there any aspects of this guide that you particularly liked? _____

_____
_____
_____

continued on next page...

Is there anything we could have done better? _____
_____
_____

About you...
Name (*Mr/Mrs/Ms*) _____
Address _____
_____
_____ Postcode _____

Daytime tel nos _____
Email _____

Please only give us your mobile phone number or email if you wish to hear from us about other products and services from the AA and partners by text or mms, or email.

Which age group are you in?
Under 25 ☐   25–34 ☐   35–44 ☐   45–54 ☐   55–64 ☐   65+ ☐

How many trips do you make a year?
Less than one ☐   One ☐   Two ☐   Three or more ☐

Are you an AA member? Yes ☐   No ☐

About your trip...
When did you book? m m / y y   When did you travel? m m / y y

How long did you stay? _____

Was it for business or leisure? _____

Did you buy any other travel guides for your trip? _____

If yes, which ones? _____
_____
_____

Thank you for taking the time to complete this questionnaire. Please send it to us as soon as possible, and remember, you do not need a stamp (*unless posted outside the UK*).

AA Travel Insurance call 0800 072 4168 or visit www.theAA.com